Everyware

The dawning age of ubiquitous computing

by Adam Greenfield

Everyware: The dawning age of ubiquitous computing
Adam Greenfield

New Riders
1249 Eighth Street
Berkeley, CA 94710
510/524-2178
800/283-9444
510/524-2221 (fax)

Published in association with AIGA

Find us on the Web at: www.newriders.com
To report errors, please send a note to errata@peachpit.com

New Riders is an imprint of Peachpit, a division of Pearson Education

Icons designed by Adam Greenfield and Nurri Kim, inspired by the work of Timo Arnall.

Project Editor: Michael J. Nolan	Compositor: Joan Olson
Development Editor: Dan Littman	Indexer: Karin Arrigoni
Production Editor: Hilal Sala	Cover design: Alicia Buelow
Copyeditor: Alan Reade	Interior design: Joan Olson

ISBN 0-321-38401-6

9 8 7 6 5 4 3

Printed and bound in the United States of America

Contents

For Nurri, just like honey

They built the world as we know it...
All the systems you traverse.

—The Fall, *I Am Kurious Oranj*

Introduction

1.

This book is an attempt to describe the form computing will take in the next few years. Specifically, it's about a vision of processing power so distributed throughout the environment that computers per se effectively disappear. It's about the enormous consequences this disappearance has for the kinds of tasks computers are applied to, for the way we use them, and for what we understand them to be.

Although aspects of this vision have been called a variety of names—ubiquitous computing, pervasive computing, physical computing, tangible media, and so on—I think of them as facets of one coherent paradigm of interaction that I call *everyware*.

In everyware, all the information we now look to our phones or Web browsers to provide becomes accessible from just about anywhere, at any time, and is delivered in a manner appropriate to our location and context.

In everyware, the garment, the room and the street become sites of processing and mediation. Household objects from shower stalls to coffee pots are reimagined as places where facts about the world can be gathered, considered, and acted upon. And all the familiar rituals of daily life—things as fundamental as the way we wake up in the morning, get to work, or shop for our groceries—are remade as an intricate dance of information about ourselves, the state of the external world, and the options available to us at any given moment.

In all of these scenarios, there are powerful informatics underlying the apparent simplicity of the experience, but they never breach the surface of awareness: things Just Work. Interactions with everyware feel natural, spontaneous, human. Ordinary people finally get to benefit from the full power of information technology, without having to absorb the esoteric bodies of knowledge on which it depends. And the sensation of use—

even while managing an unceasing and torrential flow of data—is one of calm, of relaxed mastery.

This, anyway, is the promise.

2.

The appeal of all this is easy to understand. Who wouldn't desire a technology that promised to smooth the edges of modern life, subtly intervene on our behalf to guide us when we're lost, and remind us of the things we've forgotten? Who could object to one that dispensed with the clutter of computers and other digital devices we live with, even while doing all the things they do better?

The vision is a lovely one: deeply humane, even compassionate. But getting from here to there may prove difficult. Whatever improvement we hope to achieve by overlaying our lives with digital mediation, we'll have to balance against the risk of unduly complicating that which is presently straightforward, breaking that which now works, and introducing new levels of frustration and inconvenience into all the most basic operations of our lives.

We will have to account for what happens when such mediation breaks down—as it surely will from time to time, given its origins in the same institutions, and the same development methodologies, that brought us unreliable mobile phone connections, mandatory annual operating system upgrades, and the Blue Screen of Death.

We will have to accept that privacy as we have understood it may become a thing of the past: that we will be presented the option of trading away access to the most intimate details of our lives in return for increased convenience, and that many of us will accept.

And we will have to reckon with the emergent aspects of our encounter with everyware, with all the ways in which its impact turns out to be something unforeseeably more than the sum of its parts.

What we can already see is this: everyware will surface and make explicit facts about our world that perhaps we would be happier ignoring. In countless ways, it will disturb unwritten agreements about workspace and homespace, the presentation of self and the right to privacy. It contains an inherent, unsettling potential for panoptical surveillance, regulation, and "rationalization." Its presence in our lives will transfigure our notions of space and time, self and other, citizen and society in ways that we haven't begun to contemplate.

If we pay close attention to all of these repercussions, we may conclude that everyware is something that should be approached with an unusual degree of care—more so because, on balance, we're just not very good at doing "smart." As a culture, we have so far been unable to craft high-technological artifacts that embody an understanding of the subtlety and richness of everyday life. And yet in everyware we're proposing to remake the very relations that define our lives, remodeling them on a technical paradigm nobody seems particularly satisfied with. A close reading of the existing literature on ubiquitous and pervasive systems is all that is necessary to feel the dissonance, to trip over the odd dislocations that crop up whenever we follow old maps into a new territory. We become acutely aware of our need for a more sensitive description of the terrain.

3.

We will surely need one, at any rate, if we are to make sense of the wave of change even now bearing down on us. And we will feel this need in short order, because whether we're ready for it or not, everyware is coming.

It is coming because there are too many too powerful institutions vested in its coming, knowing what enormous market possibilities are opened up by the conquest of the everyday. It is coming because it is an irresistible, "technically sweet" challenge, for designers no less than engineers. It is coming because something like it effectively became inevitable the moment our tools, products and services started communicating in ones and zeroes.

It is coming—and as yet, the people who will be most affected by it, the overwhelming majority of whom are nontechnical, nonspecialist, ordinary citizens of the developed world, barely know it even exists.

This is not due to any inherent obscurity or lack of interest in the field; to date, there have been some seven annual Ubicomp conferences, three Pervasives, and a wide scatter of smaller but otherwise similar colloquia. These are established events, in academic terms: well-attended, underwritten by companies such as Intel, Sony, Nokia and Samsung. There are at least three peer-reviewed professional journals exclusively dedicated to ubiquitous or pervasive computing. There has been no dearth of discussion of everyware...but little of this discussion, and virtually none that might offer enough information on which to build meaningful choices, has reached the mainstream.

There is a window of time before the issues we've touched upon become urgent daily realities for most of us, but it is narrowing by the day. As of this writing, "u-" for "ubiquitous" has already joined "e-" and "i-" in the parade of content-free buzz-prefixes used by the marketers of technology to connote trendiness; not a day goes by without the appearance of some relevant news item.

We hear about RFID tags being integrated into employee ID cards, a new modular sensor grid on the architectural market, a networking scheme proposing to use the body's own electrical field to carry information—and this in the general press, not the specialist journals. There's already a steady stream of prototype everyware emerging from the research labs and the more advanced corporate design studios, no matter whether they're answers to questions nobody's much asked.

With actual, consumer-facing applications (and implications) starting to appear, it's time for discussions about everyware's potential for risk and reward to leave the tight orbit of academic journals and conferences behind. If everyware hasn't yet reached its Betamax vs. VHS stage—that stage in the adoption of any new technology where the standards that will determine the particulars of its eventual shape are ironed out—we can see that it's not so terribly far off. It's time for the people who have the most at stake in the emergence of this technology to take their rightful place at the table. The challenge now is to begin thinking about how we can mold that emergence to suit our older prerogatives of personal agency, civil liberty, and simple sanity.

4.

I'm afraid that readers looking for a technical explanation of RFID tag readers, gestural interfaces, or operating systems capable of juggling the multiple, distributed events of ubiquitous environments will be sorely disappointed in this book. My intention here is simply to describe what ubiquitous computing is; establish that it is a very real concern for all of us, and in the relatively near term; explore some of the less-obvious implications of its spread as a paradigm; and finally, develop some ideas about how we might improve it.

How can we deliver the promise of everyware while forestalling some of the pitfalls that are already apparent? How can we, as users and consumers, hope to influence something that is already in the process of unfolding?

The pages to come will frame an answer to these questions. In the balance of this book, we'll explore what the emergence of robust, real-world everyware will mean, in terms useful to the designers and developers of such systems, to the marketers tasked with selling them, and to the policymakers charged with bringing them into conformance with our other agreements about the world. We'll consider some of the deeper context in which notions of everyware arise, in the hope that if we stand back far enough, we can see how all its pieces fit together, and what is implied in their joining. And we'll do this without losing sight of the individual human being encountering everyware, in the hope that what we choose to build together will prove to be useful and valuable to that person and supportive of the best that is in us.

If we make wise choices about the terms on which we accept it, we can extend the utility and convenience of ubiquitous computing to billions of lives, addressing dissatisfactions as old as human history. Or we can watch passively as the world fills up with ubiquitous systems not designed with our interests at heart—at best presenting us with moments of hassle, disruption, and frustration beyond number, and at worst laying the groundwork for the kind of repression the despots of the twentieth century could only dream about.

The stakes, this time, are unusually high. A mobile phone is something that can be switched off or left at home. A computer is something that can be shut down, unplugged, walked away from. But the technology we're discussing here—ambient, ubiquitous, capable of insinuating itself into all the apertures everyday life affords it—will form our environment in a way neither of those technologies can. There should be little doubt that its advent will profoundly shape both the world and our experience of it in the years ahead.

As to whether we come to regard that advent as boon, burden, or blunder, that is very much up to us and the decisions we make now.

A NOTE ON *Everyware*

Every argument in this book is, at root, predicated on the continuing existence and vitality of our highly energy-intensive technological civilization. This book should not be construed as a statement of belief that our current way of life is in fact sustainable.

Acknowledgments

The three greatest friends this book ever had have been Liz Danzico, Howard Rheingold and Christina Wodtke. Very simply, *Everyware* would not exist without their influence; my gratitude to them is immense. I would also like to thank Peter Morville and Jeffrey Zeldman for their crucial early enthusiasm.

At Peachpit, Nancy Aldrich-Ruenzel showed extraordinary faith in my vision for this book, affording me leeway few authors ever enjoy; I was both moved and inspired. I would like to thank Marjorie Baer, Michael Nolan and Camille Peri for their insightful and untiring efforts on behalf of this book.

I would particularly like to thank my editor, Dan Littman, for being a stickler when I needed him to be, and indulging me otherwise. *Everyware* is immeasurably better for his exertions.

I owe untold debts of gratitude to my wonderful hosts: at the University of Oslo's InterMedia program, Andrew Morrison and Idunn Sem; Spreeblick's Johnny Haeusler and Tanja Kreitschmann; at Ci'Num, Marcel Desvergne, and, at Aquitaine Europe Communication, Hervé Le Guyader, Thierry Ulmet, Frédéric Autechaud and their entire event-planning staff. In every case, they made me feel more like family than guest.

My thanks to Victoria Bellotti, Leo Fernekes, Christian Kray, Nicolas Nova, and David Small for their assistance in clarifying certain details of the text.

I could not have written a word without a very good set of earphones and the 4,758 tracks I have in iTunes, especially the music of Alarm Will Sound, Amon Tobin, Do Make Say Think, Brian Eno, Four Tet, Godspeed You Black Emperor!, the various incarnations of John Zorn's Masada, Mogwai, Michael Nyman, Arvo Pärt, and Sigur Rös...leavened by the occasional hit of Stooges. I was equally dependent on the Rose Reading Room of the

New York Public Library, where most of *Everyware* was written, and the circa-1961 Swan chair I sat in while writing most of the rest.

Yasmine Abbas, Rachel Abrams, Timo Arnall, Paul Baron, Pete Barr-Watson, Gene Becker, Wayne Berkowitz, Carrie Bickner, Rebecca Blood, Bryan Boyer, Abe Burmeister, Ben Cerveny, Michele Chang, Jan Chipchase, Tom Coates, Eric Culnaert, Alan Dix, John Emerson, Jyri Engeström, Daniel Erasmus, Chris Fahey, Jim Faris, Naoto Fukasawa, Raye Fukuda, Anne Galloway, Liz Goodman, Kelly Goto, Steve Graff, Raphael Grignani, Chris Heathcote, Anna Henckel-Donnersmarck, Dan Hill, Steph Hügel, Mimi Ito, Matt Jones, Younghee Jung, Gen Kanai, Nurri Kim, Daniel Kaplan, Dirk Knemeyer, Mike Kuniavsky, Ranjit Makkuni, Joe McCarthy, Mike Migurski, Craig Mod, Jamie Mowder, Herbert Muschamp, Ulla-Maaria Mutanen, Andrew Otwell, Chris Palmieri, John Poisson, Odd-Wiking Rahlff, Eric Rodenbeck, Celia Romaniuk, Fabio Sergio, Carsten Schwesig, Jack Schulze, Steve Silberman, Kevin Slavin, Molly Wright Steenson, John Thackara, Thomas Vander Wal, Matt Ward, Matt Webb, Even Westvang, Daniel Wolpert and John Zapolski were instrumental in helping me formulate my ideas, whether they knew it or not.

While they must be held blameless for any errors in fact, emphasis or judgment—all of which are of course my own—their influence on this book is impossible to overstate. I thank them for the fellowship, the conversations and the wonderful memories, across three years and an equal number of continents.

I'd also like to thank my loyal readership at v-2.org, and Amy Hammersmith, Ian Jacobs, Anthony Leone, Jamie Mowder and Sharon Stark for their enduring friendship, without which no writer can survive.

My wife Nurri Kim has always been my fiercest advocate and toughest critic. She is the core of my life and beacon of my days.

And finally, I want to thank my mother, father, and sister, for the fact that I grew up in a house of words, ideas, and loving challenges. There can be no overstating the magnitude of this gift, and in a very deep sense, every word I write belongs to them.

SECTION 1

What is everyware?

Ever more pervasive, ever harder to perceive, computing has leapt off the desktop and insinuated itself into everyday life. Such ubiquitous information technology "everyware"—will appear in many different contexts and take a wide variety of forms, but it will affect almost every one of us, whether we're aware of it or not.

What is everyware? How can we recognize it when we encounter it? And how can we expect it to show up in our lives?

Thesis 01

There are many ubiquitous computings.

Almost twenty years ago, a researcher at the legendary Xerox Palo Alto Research Center wrote an article—a sketch, really—setting forth the outlines of what computing would look like in a post-PC world.

The researcher's name was Mark Weiser, and his thoughts were summarized in a brief burst simply entitled "Ubiquitous Computing #1." In it, as in the series of seminal papers and articles that followed, Weiser developed the idea of an "invisible" computing, a computing that "does not live on a personal device of any sort, but is in the woodwork everywhere."

What Weiser was describing would be nothing less than computing without computers. In his telling, desktop machines per se would largely disappear, as the tiny, cheap microprocessors that powered them faded into the built environment. But *computation* would flourish, becoming intimately intertwined with the stuff of everyday life.

In this context, "ubiquitous" meant not merely "in every place," but also "in every thing." Ordinary objects, from coffee cups to raincoats to the paint on the walls, would be reconsidered as sites for the sensing and processing of information, and would wind up endowed with surprising new properties. Best of all, people would interact with these systems fluently and naturally, barely noticing the powerful informatics they were engaging. The innumerable hassles presented by personal computing would fade into history.

Even for an institution already famed for paradigm-shattering innovations—the creation of the graphical user interface and the Ethernet networking protocol notable among them—Weiser's "ubicomp" stood out as an unusually bold vision. But while the line of thought he developed at PARC may have offered the first explicit, technically articulated formulation of a ubiquitous computing in the post-PC regime, it wasn't the only one. The general idea of an invisible-but-everywhere computing was clearly loose in the world.

At the MIT Media Lab, Professor Hiroshi Ishii's "Things That Think" initiative developed interfaces bridging the realms of bits and atoms, a "tangible media" extending computation out into the walls and doorways of everyday experience. At IBM, a whole research group grew up around a "pervasive computing" of smart objects, embedded sensors, and the always-on networks that connected them.

And as mobile phones began to percolate into the world, each of them nothing but a connected computing device, it was inevitable that someone would think to use them as a platform for the delivery of services beyond conversation. Philips and Samsung, Nokia and NTT DoCoMo— all offered visions of a mobile, interconnected computing in which, naturally, their products took center stage.

By the first years of the twenty-first century, with daily reality sometimes threatening to leapfrog even the more imaginative theorists of ubicomp, it was clear that all of these endeavors were pointing at something becoming real in the world.

Intriguingly, though, and maybe a little infuriatingly, none of these institutions understood the problem domain in quite the same way. In their attempts to grapple with the implications of computing in the post-PC era, some concerned themselves with *ubiquitous networking:* the effort to extend network access to just about anyplace people could think of to go. With available Internet addresses dwindling by the day, this required the development of a new-generation Internet protocol; it also justified the efforts of companies ranging from Intel to GM to LG to imagine an array of "smart" consumer products designed with that network in mind.

Others concentrated on the engineering details of instrumenting physical space. In the late 1990s, researchers at UC Berkeley developed a range of wireless-enabled, embedded sensors and microcontrollers known generically as *motes*, as well as an operating system for them to run on. All were specifically designed for use in ubicomp,

Thirty miles to the south, a team at Stanford addressed the absence in orthodox computer science of a infrastructural model appropriate for the ubiquitous case. In 2002, they published a paper describing the *event heap*, a way of allocating computational resources that better accounted for the arbitrary comings and goings of multiple simultaneous users than did the traditional "event queue."

Developments elsewhere in the broader information technology field had clear implications for the ubiquitous model. *Radio-frequency identi- fication (RFID) tags* and *two-dimensional barcodes* were just two of many technologies adapted from their original applications, pressed into ser- vice in ubicomp scenarios as bridges between the physical and virtual worlds. Meanwhile, at the human-machine interface, the plummeting cost of processing resources meant that long-dreamed-of but compu- tationally-intensive ways of interaction, such as *gesture recognition* and *voice recognition*, were becoming practical; they would prove irresistible as elements of a technology that was, after all, supposed to be invisible- but-everywhere.

And beyond that, there was clearly a ferment at work in many of the fields touching on ubicomp, even through the downturn that followed the crash of the "new economy" in early 2001. It had reached something like a critical mass of thought and innovation by 2005: an upwelling of nov- elty both intellectual and material, accompanied by a persistent sense, in many quarters, that ubicomp's hour had come 'round at last. Pieces of the puzzle kept coming. By the time I began doing the research for this book, the literature on ubicomp was a daily tide of press releases and new papers that was difficult to stay on top of: papers on *wearable com- puting, augmented reality, locative media, near-field communication, body- area networking*. In many cases, the fields were so new that the jargon hadn't even solidified yet.

Would all of these threads converge on something comprehensible, useful, or usable? Would any of these ubiquitous computings fulfill PARC's promise of a "calm technology?" And if so, how?

Questions like these were taken up with varying degrees of enthusiasm, skepticism, and critical distance in the overlapping *human-computer interaction* (HCI) and *user experience* (UX) communities. The former, with an academic engineering pedigree, had evolved over some thirty years to consider the problems inherent in any encounter between complex technical systems and the people using them; the latter, a more or less ad hoc network of practitioners, addressed similar concerns in their daily work, as the Internet and the World Wide Web built on it became facts of life for millions of nonspecialist users. As the new millennium dawned, both communities found ubicomp on their agendas, in advance of any hard data gleaned from actual use.

With the exception of discussions going on in the HCI community, none of these groups were necessarily pursuing anything that Mark Weiser would have recognized as fully cognate with his ubiquitous computing. But they were all sensing the rapidly approaching obsolescence of the desktop model, the coming hegemony of networked devices, and the reconfiguration of everyday life around them. What they were all grasping after, each in their own way, was a language of interaction suited to a world where information processing would be everywhere in the human environment.

Thesis 02

The many forms of ubiquitous computing are indistinguishable from the user's perspective and will appear to a user as aspects of a single paradigm: everyware.

In considering Mark Weiser's "ubiquitous" computing alongside all those efforts that define the next computing as one that is "mobile" or "wearable" or "connected" or "situated," one is reminded time and again of the parable of the six blind men describing an elephant.

We've all heard this one, haven't we? Six wise elders of the village were asked to describe the true nature of the animal that had been brought before them; sadly, age and infirmity had reduced them all to a reliance on the faculty of touch. One sage, trying and failing to wrap his arms around the wrinkled circumference of the beast's massive leg, replied that it must surely be among the mightiest of trees. Another discerned a great turtle in the curving smoothness of a tusk, while yet another, encountering the elephant's sinuous, muscular trunk, thought he could hardly have been handling anything other than the king of snakes. None of the six, in fact, could come anywhere close to agreement regarding what it was that they were experiencing, and their disagreement might have become quite acrimonious had the village idiot not stepped in to point out that they were all in the presence of the same creature.

And so it is with post-PC computing. Regardless of the valid distinctions between these modes, technologies, and strategies, I argue that such distinctions are close to meaningless from the perspective of people exposed to the computing these theories all seem to describe.

Historically, there have been some exceptions to the general narrowness of vision in the field. Hiroshi Ishii's Tangible Media Group at the MIT Media Lab saw their work as cleaving into three broad categories: "interactive surfaces," in which desks, walls, doors, and even ceilings were reimagined as input/output devices; "ambients," which used phenomena such as sound, light, and air currents as peripheral channels to the user; and "tangibles," which leveraged the "graspable and manipulable" qualities of physical objects as provisions of the human interface.

A separate MIT effort, Project Oxygen, proceeded under the assumption that a coherently pervasive presentation would require coordinated effort at all levels; they set out to design a coordinated suite of devices and user interfaces, sensor grids, software architecture, and ad hoc and mesh-network strategies. (Nobody could accuse them of lacking ambition.)

These inclusive visions aside, however, very few of the people working in ubicomp or its tributaries seem to have quite gotten how all these pieces would fit together. From the user's point of view, I'd argue, these are all facets of a single larger experience.

What is that experience? It involves a diverse ecology of devices and platforms, most of which have nothing to do with "computers" as we've understood them. It's a distributed phenomenon: The power and meaning we ascribe to it are more a property of the network than of any single node, and that network is effectively invisible. It permeates places and pursuits that we've never before thought of in technical terms. And it is something that happens out here in the world, amid the bustle, the traffic, the lattes, and gossip: a social activity shaped by, and in its turn shaping, our relationships with the people around us.

And although too many changes in the world get called "paradigm shifts"—the phrase has been much abused in our time—when we consider the difference between our experience of PCs and the thing that is coming, it is clear that in this case no other description will do. Its sense of a technological transition entraining a fundamental alteration in worldview, and maybe even a new state of being, is fully justified.

We need a new word to begin discussing the systems that make up this state of being—a word that is deliberately vague enough that it collapses all of the inessential distinctions in favor of capturing the qualities they all have in common.

What can we call this paradigm? I think of it as *everyware*.

Thesis 03

**Everyware is information processing embedded in
the objects and surfaces of everyday life.**

Part of what the everyware paradigm implies is that most of the functionality we now associate with these boxes on our desks, these slabs that
warm our laps, will be dispersed into both the built environment and the
wide variety of everyday objects we typically use there.

Many such objects are already invested with processing power—most
contemporary cameras, watches, and phones, to name the most obvious examples, contain microcontrollers. But we understand these things
to be technical, and if they have so far rarely participated in the larger
conversation of the "Internet of things," we wouldn't necessarily be surprised to see them do so.

Nor are we concerned, for the moment, with the many embedded microprocessors we encounter elsewhere in our lives, generally without being
aware of them. They pump the brakes in our cars, cycle the compres-
sors in our refrigerators, or adjust the water temperature in our washing machines, yet never interact with the wider universe. They can't be
queried or addressed by remote systems, let alone interact directly with
a human user.

It's not until they do share the stream of information passing through
them with other applications and services that they'll become of interest
to us. It is my sense that the majority of embedded systems will eventually link up with broader networks, but for now they play a relatively small
role in our story.

By contrast, what we're contemplating here is the extension of informa-
tion-sensing, -processing, and -networking capabilities to entire classes

of things we've never before thought of as "technology." At least, we haven't thought of them that way in a long, long time: I'm talking about artifacts such as clothing, furniture, walls and doorways.

Their transparency is precisely why this class of objects is so appealing to engineers and designers as platforms for computation. These things are already everywhere, hiding in plain sight; nobody bats an eyelash at them. If nothing else, they offer a convenient place to stash the componentry of a computing power that might otherwise read as oppressive. More ambitiously, as we'll see, some designers are exploring how the possibilities inherent in an everyday object can be thoroughly transformed by the application of information technologies like RFID, Global Positioning System (GPS), and mesh networking.

The idea of incorporating digital "intelligence" into objects with an everyday form factor—industrial-designer jargon for an object's physical shape and size—appeared early in the developmental history of ubicomp. As far back as 1989, Olivetti Research deployed an early version of Roy Want's Active Badge, in which the familiar workplace identity tag became a platform for functionality.

Workers wearing Active Badges in an instrumented building could automatically unlock areas to which they had been granted access, have phone calls routed to them wherever they were, and create running diaries of the meetings they attended. They could also be tracked as they moved around the building; at one point, Olivetti's public Web site even allowed visitors to query the location of an employee wearing an Active Badge. And while the intent wasn't to spy on such workers, it was readily apparent how the system could be abused, especially when the device responsible was so humble and so easy to forget about. Original sin came early to ubicomp.

Want went on to join Mark Weiser's team at PARC (Palo Alto Research Center), where he contributed to foundational work on a range of networked devices called "tabs," "pads," and "boards." As with Active Badge, these were digital tools for freely roaming knowledge workers, built on a vocabulary of form universally familiar to anyone who's ever worked in an office: name tags, pads of paper, and erasable whiteboards, respectively.*

Each had a recognizable domain of function. Tabs, being the smallest, were also the most personal; they stayed close to the body, where they might mediate individual information such as identity, location and availability. Pads were supposed to be an individual's primary work surface, pen-based devices for documents and other personal media. And boards were wall-sized displays through which personal work could be shared, in a flow of discovery, annotation and commentary.

Networking infrastructure throughout the office itself enabled communication among the constellation of tabs, pads and boards in active use, allocating shared resources like printers, routing incoming e-mails and phone calls, and providing background maintenance and security functions. Documents in progress would follow a worker into and out of meetings, up onto public boards for discussion, and back down to one's own pad for further revision.

Part of the reasoning behind this was to replace the insular, socially alienating PC with something that afforded the same productivity. In this, PARC anticipated by half a decade the casual, and casually technical, workspace that did in fact emerge during the late-1990s ascendancy of the dot-coms. At least in theory, by getting people out from behind their screens, tabs and pads and boards lent themselves to an open, fluid, and collaborative work style.

Although none of these devices was ever commercialized, at least by Xerox, the die had been cast. Many of the ubicomp projects that followed took PARC's assumptions more or less as givens, as researchers turned

---

*These form factors had been looming in the mass unconscious for a long time. PARC's "pad," in particular, seemed to owe a lot to the slablike media/communication devices used by astronauts Frank Poole and Dave Bowman in Stanley Kubrick's 1968 classic 2001: A Space Odyssey.

their efforts toward enabling the vision of collaborative, distributed work embedded in it.

But what about that percentage of our lives we spend outside the confines of work? While it was more or less inevitable that efforts would be made to provision objects outside the workplace with a similar capacity for digital mediation—if for no other reason than the attractively high margins and immense volume of the consumer-electronics sector—it took longer for them to appear.

To understand why such efforts took so long to get off the ground, it's necessary to reconstruct for a moment what the world looked like at the very dawn of ubicomp. As strange as it now seems, the early conceptual work in the field happened in a world without a Web or, for that matter, widespread adoption of mobile phones in North America.

The 802.11b standard we know as Wi-Fi, of course, didn't yet exist. You couldn't simply cobble together a project around off-the-shelf wireless routers. The in-building wireless network prototypes like Active Badge depended on were bespoke, one-off affairs; in more than one project, students simply sketched in connectivity as a black box, an assertion that *if* an actual network were somehow to come into existence, *then* the proposed system would function like so.

In such an environment, it may have been reasonable to posit a pervasive wireless network in the workplace. However, a deployment in public space or the domestic sphere was clearly out of the question.

The mass uptake of the Internet changed everything. What would have seemed fanciful from the perspective of 1992 became far more credible in its wake. As a lingua franca, as an enabling technology, and especially as an available kit of parts, the dramatic, global spread of Internet Protocol-based networking immediately made schemes of ubiquity feasible.

Over the next several years, a profusion of projects explored various strategies for living with, and not merely using, information technology. Some of the proposals and products we'll be encountering in this book include keys and wallets that locate themselves when misplaced; a beer mat that summons the bartender when an empty mug is placed upon it; and a bathtub that sounds a tone in another room when the desired water temperature has been reached.*

Some of the most beautiful everyware I've seen was designed by former PARC researcher Ranjit Makkuni, whose New Delhi-based Sacred World Foundation works to bridge the gap between technological and traditional cultures. This is information processing interwoven with the familiar daily forms not of the developed world, but of the global South, cycle rickshaws, clay pots, and amulets among them. It's a lovely reminder that the world contains a great many different "everydays," beyond the ones we happen to be used to.

Whether clay pot or beer mat, though, these projects all capitalize on the idea that the distinctly local application of intelligence, and not the generic, one-size-fits-all vision embodied in computers, will turn out to be among the most important and useful legacies of our technological moment. In this, they appear to be following the advice of human interface pioneer Don Norman.

Norman argues, in *The Invisible Computer* and elsewhere, that the difficulty and frustration we experience in using the computer are primarily artifacts of its general-purpose nature. He proposes that a truly human-centered design would explode the computer's many functions into a "quiet, invisible, unobtrusive" array of networked objects scattered throughout the home: simple, single-purpose "information appliances" in the form of shoes, bookshelves, even teddy bears.

Or we could go still deeper "into the woodwork." Stefano Marzano points out, in his introduction to Philips Electronics' 2000 exploration of wearable electronics, *New Nomads*, that when we remove the most transient layer of things from the environments we spend our lives in, we're

---

Could the mental models attached to such familiar forms unduly limit what people think of to do with them? The answer is almost certainly yes; we'll take up that question a bit later on.

left with nothing but the spaces themselves, abstracted down to their essentials. These are universals humans have lived in for millennia, elements like walls and roofs, tables and seating, clothing. And, of course, the body itself—our original and our final home. In everyware, all of these present appealing platforms for networked computation.

Fifteen years downstream from its tentative beginnings at Olivetti, the idea of the ordinary as a new frontier for computing is finally starting to bear fruit. We're beginning to see the walls and books, sweaters, and tabletops around us reconsidered as sensors, interface objects, or active sites that respond in some way to data they receive from outside. Eventually, we may even come to see them as the articulated parts of a massively distributed computational engine.

When everyday things are endowed with the ability to sense their environment, store metadata reflecting their own provenance, location, status, and use history, and share that information with other such objects, this cannot help but redefine our relationship with such things. We'll find our daily experience of the world altered in innumerable ways, some obvious and some harder to discern. And among the more significant consequences of this "computing everywhere" is that it strongly implies "information everywhere."

Thesis 04

Everyware gives rise to a regime of ambient informatics.

With its provisions for sensing capacity built into such a wide variety of everyday objects, we've seen that everyware multiplies by many, many times the number of places in the world in which information can be gathered. The global network will no longer be fed simply by keyboards, microphones, and cameras, in other words, but also by all of the inputs implied by the pervasive deployment of computational awareness.

Even if all of those new inputs were fed into conventional outputs—Web sites, say, or infographics on the evening news—that would certainly be a significant evolution in the way we experience the world. But everyware also provides for a far greater diversity of channels through which information can be expressed, either locally or remotely. In addition to relatively ordinary displays, it offers spoken notifications, "earcons" and other audio cues; changes in light level or color; even alterations in the physical qualities of objects and architectural surfaces, from temperature to reflectivity.

And it's this expansion in the available modes of output that is likely to exert a much stronger shaping influence on our lives. When so many more kinds of information can be expressed just about anywhere, the practical effect will be to bring about a relationship with that information that I think of as *ambient informatics*.

Ambient informatics is a state in which information is freely available at the point in space and time someone requires it, generally to support a specific decision. Maybe it's easiest simply to describe it as information detached from the Web's creaky armature of pages, sites, feeds and browsers, and set free instead in the wider world to be accessed when, how and where you want it.

One of the notions that arrives alongside ambient informatics is the idea of context- or location-aware services. This could be something as simple as a taxi's rooftop advertisement cross-referencing current GPS coordinates with a database of bank branches, in order to display the location of the nearest ATM. It could be the hackneyed m-commerce use case, all but invariably trotted out in these discussions, of a discount "coupon" sent to your phone whenever you pass through the catchment area of a Starbucks or a McDonald's. Or it might simply mean that the information pushed to you varies with where you are, who you're with, and what you're doing.

Ideally, this means effortless utility—the day's weather displayed on your bathroom mirror, the traffic report on your windshield, the cue embedded in your wallet or handbag that lets you know when one of your friends is within a hundred meters of your present position—but, as we shall see, there are darker implications as well. Perhaps we'll find that a world with too much information presents as many problems as one with too little.

Either way, there will still be an Internet, and we'll likely make more use of it than ever before. But with contextual information diffused as appropriate in the environment, we won't need a computer to get to it, and the entire Web as we've come to know it may become something of a backwater.

Thesis 05

At its most refined, everyware can be understood as information processing dissolving in behavior.

The great product designer Naoto Fukasawa speaks of "design dissolving in behavior." By this, he means interactions with designed systems so well thought out by their authors, and so effortless on the part of their users, that they effectively abscond from awareness.

The objects he is best known for—mobile phones and CD players, humidifiers and television sets, uniformly display this quality. His work draws much of its power from its attention to the subtle, humble, profoundly comfortable ways in which people use the world—the unconsciousness with which people hang umbrellas from a lunch counter by their handles, use notepads as impromptu drink coasters, or gaze at their reflections in a mug of coffee. There's a lot in common here with Mark Weiser's dictum that "the most profound technologies are those that disappear."

Correspondingly, we can think of everyware as information processing dissolving in behavior. This is the ambition that I discern behind so many of the scenarios of ubiquitous and pervasive computing, from Roy Want to Don Norman: that we could claim the best of both worlds, harnessing all of the power of a densely networked environment, but refining its perceptible signs until they disappear into the things we do every day.

In this telling, ordinary interactions with information become transparent, eliminating the needless deformations introduced by our forty-year fixation on "the computer." You close the door to your office because you want privacy, and your phone and IM channel are automatically set to "unavailable." You point to an unfamiliar word in a text, and a definition appears. You sit down to lunch with three friends, and the restaurant plays only music that you've all rated highly. In each scenario, powerful informatics intervene to produce the experience, but you'd have to look pretty hard to turn up their traces. Such interactions are supposed to feel natural, human, *right*.

Well and good, in principle. How does it work in practice? Let's take a canonical example: the exchange of business cards.

This tiny ritual happens by the million every day, throughout the commercial world. The practice differs from place to place, but it is always important, always symbolically freighted with performances of status and power, or accessibility and openness. It's no stretch to assert that billion-dollar deals have hinged on this exchange of tokens. How could it be reimagined as everyware?

One, relatively crude and timid, expression might propose that, instead of the inert slips of paper we now proffer, we hand out RFID-equipped "smart" cards encoding our contact information and preferences. (Maybe you'd tap such a card against a reader to place a call, without having to be bothered with the details of remembering a number, or even a full name; fans of *Aliens* may recall that Lt. Ripley availed herself of just such an interface, in her wee-hours call to corporate weasel Burke.)

In a more aggressive version of this story the physical token disappears from the transaction; instead, a data file containing the same information is transmitted from one party to the other over a low-voltage network, using the skin's own inherent conductivity. Maybe, in a further refinement, the only data actually sent over the network is a pointer, a key to unlock a record maintained locally elsewhere.

And there it is, everyware's true and perfect sigil. Information has passed between two parties, adding a node to one's personal or professional network. This transaction takes several steps to accomplish on a contemporary social-networking site, and here it's been achieved with a simple handshake—an act externally indistinguishable from its non-enhanced equivalent. Here we can truly begin to understand what Weiser may have been thinking when he talked about "disappearance."

If that's too abstract for you, let's take a look at MasterCard's RFID-equipped PayPass contactless payment system, which will have been introduced commercially (alongside Chase's packaging of it as Blink) by the time this book is published. MasterCard's tagline for PayPass is "tap & go," but that belies the elaborate digital choreography concealed behind the simple, appealing premise.

Schematically, it looks like this: You bring your card, key fob, or other PayPass-equipped object into range, by tapping it on the reader's "landing zone." The reader feeds power inductively to the device's embedded antenna, which powers the chip. The chip responds by transmitting an encrypted stream of data corresponding to your account number, a stream produced by modulating the strength of the electromagnetic field between it and the reader.

From this point forward, the transaction proceeds in the conventional manner: the reader queries the network for authorization, compares the amount of the purchase in question with the availability of funds on hand, and confirms or denies the purchase. And all of that happens in the space of 0.2 seconds: far less than a single heartbeat, and, as MasterCard clearly counts on, not nearly enough time to consider the ramifications of what we've just done.

Intel Research's Elizabeth Goodman argues that, "[t]he promise of computing technology dissolving into behavior, invisibly permeating the natural world around us cannot be reached," because "technology is...that which by definition is separate from the natural." In the face of technologies like PayPass, though, I wonder whether she's right. I don't think it's at all unlikely that such transactions will effectively become invisible—at least, for most of us, most of the time.

I do, however, think it's of concern. If this dissolving into behavior is the Holy Grail of a calm and unobtrusive computing, it's also the crux of so many of the other issues which ought to unsettle us—simultaneously everyware's biggest promise, and its greatest challenge.

Thesis 06

There are many rationales for the move away from the PC, any one of which would have been sufficient on its own.

At this point, you may well be wondering about the "why" of all this. Why embed computing in everyday objects? Why reinvent thoroughly assimilated habits and behaviors around digital mediation? Above all, why give up the settled and familiar context of the PC for a wild and unruly user environment, rivaling in complexity the knottiest and most difficult problems human beings have ever set up for themselves?

As you might suspect, there's no one answer. Part of the reason that the emergence of everyware seems so inevitable to me is that there are a great many technical, social, and economic forces driving it, any one of which would probably have been sufficient on its own.

Certainly, Mark Weiser's contingent at PARC wanted to push computation into the environment because they hoped that doing so judiciously might ameliorate some less pleasant aspects of a user experience that constantly threatened to spin out of control. As Weiser and co-author John Seely Brown laid out in a seminal paper, "The Coming Age of Calm Technology," they wanted to design tools to "encalm as well as inform." Similar lines of argument can be adduced in the work of human-centered design proponents from Don Norman onward.

Much of the Japanese work along ubiquitous lines, and in parallel endeavors such as robotics, is driven by the recognition that an aging population will require not merely less complicated interfaces, but outboard memory augmentation—and Japan is far from the only place with graying demographics. Gregory Abowd's Aware Home initiative at Georgia Tech is probably the best-known effort to imagine a ubicomp that lets the elderly safely and comfortably "age in place."

Ranjit Makkuni might argue that well-crafted tangible interfaces are not merely less intimidating to the non-technically inclined but are, in fact, essential if we want to provide for the needs of the world's billion or more non-literate citizens.

The prospect of so many new (and new kinds of) sensors cannot help but beguile those groups and individuals, ever with us, whose notions of safety—or business models—hinge on near-universal surveillance. Law-enforcement and public-safety organizations planetwide can be numbered among them, as well as the ecosystem of vendors, consultants, and other private concerns that depend on them for survival.

Beyond these, it would already be hard to number the businesses fairly salivating over all of the niches, opportunities, and potential revenue streams opened up by everyware.

Finally, looming behind all of these points of view is an evolution in the material and economic facts of computing. When computational resources become so cheap that there's no longer any need to be parsimonious with them, people feel freer to experiment with them. They'll be more likely to indulge "what if" scenarios: what if we network this room? this parka? this surfboard? (and inevitably: this dildo?)

With so many pressures operating in everyware's favor, it shouldn't surprise us if some kind of everyware appeared in our lives at the very first moment in which the necessary technical wherewithal existed. And that is exactly what is now happening all around us, if we only have the eyes to see it.

Whether you see this as a paradigm shift in the history of information technology, as I do, or as something more gently evolutionary, there can be little doubt that something worthy of note is happening.

Thesis 07

Everyware isn't so much a particular kind of hardware or software as it is a situation.

The difficult thing to come to terms with, when we're so used to thinking of "computing" as something to do with discrete devices, is that everyware finally isn't so much a particular kind of hardware, philosophy of software design, or set of interface conventions as it is a situation—a set of circumstances.

Half the battle of making sense of this situation is learning to recognize when we've entered it. This is especially true because so much of what makes up everyware is "invisible" by design; we have to learn to recognize the role of everyware in a "smart" hotel room, a contactless payment system, and a Bluetooth-equipped snowboarding parka.

The one consistent thread that connects all of these applications is that the introduction of information processing has wrought some gross change in their behavior or potential. And yet it appears in a different guise in each of them. Sometimes everyware is just there: an ambient, environmental, enveloping field of information. At other times, it's far more instrumental, something that a user might consciously take up and turn to an end. And it's this slippery, protean quality that can make everyware so difficult to pin down and discuss.

Nevertheless, I hope I've persuaded you by now that there is in fact a coherent "it" to be considered, something that appears whenever there are multiple computing devices devoted to each human user; when this processing power is deployed throughout local physical reality instead of being locked up in a single general-purpose box; and when interacting with it is largely a matter of voice, touch, and gesture, interwoven with the existing rituals of everyday life.

We might go a step further: The diversity of ways in which everyware will appear in our lives—as new qualities in the things that surround us, as a regime of ambient informatics, and as information processing dissolving in behavior—are linked not merely by a technical armature, but by a set of assumptions about the proper role of technology.

They're certainly different assumptions from the ones most of us have operated under for the last twenty or so years. The conceptual models we've been given to work with, both as designers of information technology and as users of it, break down completely in the face of the next computing.

As designers, we will have to develop an exquisite and entirely unprecedented sensitivity to contexts we've hitherto safely been able to ignore. As users, we will no longer be able to hold computing at arm's length, as something we're "not really interested in," whatever our predilections should happen to be. For better or worse, the everyware situation is one we all share.

Thesis 08

The project of everyware is nothing less than the colonization of everyday life by information technology.

Objects, surfaces, gestures, behaviors: as we've seen, all have become fair game for technological intervention. Considered one by one, each intervention may proceed by granular and minuscule steps, but in the aggregate, whether intentionally or not, the effect is to begin overwriting the features of our day-to-day existence with something that never used to be there.

We all have an idea what "everyday life" means, though of course the details will be different for each of us. Your conception might be organized around work: rushing to catch the train, delivering a convincing presentation to your colleagues, and remembering to pick up the dry cleaning on the way home. Someone else's might reside primarily in frustrations like paying the phone bill, or waiting in stalled traffic on the freeway.

My own sense of everyday life resides in less stressful moments, like strolling through the neighborhood after dinner with my wife, meeting friends for a drink, or simply gazing out the window onto the life of the city. However the overall tenor diverges, though, we have this much in common: We all know what it's like to bathe and dress, eat and socialize, make homes and travel between them.

Our lives are built from basic, daily operations like these. We tend to think of them as being somehow interstitial to the real business of a life, but we wind up spending much of our time on earth engaged in them. And it's precisely these operations that everyware proposes to usefully augment, out here in the rough-and-tumble of ordinary existence, in what I've elsewhere called "the brutal regime of the everyday." It aims to address questions as humble, and as important, as "Where did I leave my keys?" "Will I be warm enough in this jacket?" and "What's the best way to drive to work this morning?"

As unheroic as they are, the transactions of everyday life would hardly seem to require technical intervention. It seems strange to think of managing them through an interface of digital mediation, or indeed applying any technology beyond the most basic to their enrichment. And yet that is where computing currently appears to be headed.

The stakes are high. But troublingly—especially given the narrow window of time we have in which to make meaningful choices about the shape of everyware—a comprehensive understanding of what the options before us really mean has been hard to come by.

In the rest of this book, we'll attempt to offer just that. We'll start by examining how everyware differs from the information technology we've become accustomed to. We'll prise out, in some detail, what is driving its emergence and try to get a handle on some of the most pressing issues it confronts us with. We'll sum it all up by asking who gets to determine the shape of everyware's unfolding, how soon we need to be thinking about it, and finally, and perhaps most importantly, what we can do to improve the chance that as it appears, it does so in ways congenial to us.

How is everyware different from what we're used to?

In Section 1, we discussed the idea that a paradigm shift in the way we use computing is upon us. In its fullest sense, this shift is both an exodus from the PC as a stand-alone platform and a remaking of everyday life around the possibilities of information processing.

But how, specifically, is this different from the computing we've gotten used to? What does everyware look like from the other side of the transition?

Thesis 09

Everyware has profoundly different implications for the user experience than previous paradigms.

Contemporary designers of digital products and services speak of the "user experience": in other words, how does it feel to use this?

Where complex technological artifacts are concerned, such experiences arise from the interplay of a great many factors, subjective ones and those which are more objectively quantifiable. Consistently eliciting good user experiences means accounting for the physical design of the human interface, the flow of interaction between user and device, and the larger context in which that interaction is embedded.

In not a single one of these dimensions is the experience of everyware anything like that of personal computing. Simply put, people engaging everyware will find it hard to relate it to anything they may have experienced in previous encounters with computing technology.

Let's compare a familiar scenario from personal computing with a correspondingly typical use case for everyware to see why this is so.

The conventional case is something that happens millions of times a day: Driven by some specific need, a user sits down at her desk, opens up her computer, and launches an application—a spreadsheet, a word processor, an e-mail client. Via the computer's operating system, she issues explicit commands to that application, and with any luck she achieves what she set out to do in some reasonable amount of time.

By contrast, in everyware, a routine scenario might specify that, by entering a room, you trigger a cascade of responses on the part of embedded systems around you. Sensors in the flooring register your presence, your needs are inferred (from the time of day, the presence of others, or even the state of your own body), and conditions in the room altered accordingly. But few if any of these are directly related to the reason you had in your mind for moving from one place to another.

The everyware scenario is still based on the same primitives the desktop interaction relies upon; at the very lowest level, both are built on a similar substrate of microprocessors, memory, networking, and code. But should you happen to distribute those processors in the physical environment, link them to a grid of embedded sensors and effectors, and connect them all as nodes of a wireless network, you have something markedly different on your hands.

The PC user actively chose the time, manner, and duration of her involvement with her machine, and also (assuming that the machine was portable) had some say regarding where it took place. That one machine was the only technical system she needed to accomplish her goal, and conversely she was the only person whose commands it needed to attend to. Thus bounded on both sides, the interaction fell into a call-and-response rhythm: user actions followed by system events. In a way, we might even say that an application is called into being by the user's task-driven or information-seeking behavior and shut down when her success conditions have been achieved.

Compare these facets of the experience to the situation of everyware, in which the system precedes the user. You walk into a room, and something happens in response: The lights come on, your e-mails are routed to a local wall screen, a menu of options corresponding to your new location appears on the display sewn into your left sleeve. Maybe the response is something you weren't even aware of. Whether or not you walk into the room in pursuance of a particular aim or goal, the system's reaction to your arrival is probably tangential to that goal. Such an interaction can't meaningfully be constructed as "task-driven." Nor does anything in this interplay between user and system even correspond with the other main mode we see in human interaction with conventional computing systems: information seeking.

Could you use everyware instrumentally, to accomplish a discrete task or garner facts about the world? Of course. But that's not what it's "for," not in the same way that a specific function is what an application or a search engine is for. It simply "is," in a way that personal computing is not, and that quality necessarily evokes an entirely different kind of experience on the part of those encountering it.

Even the ways that you address such a system, or are kept apprised of its continuing operation, are different than the ones we're used to. As PARC's Victoria Bellotti and her co-authors pointed out, in a 2002 paper, designers of user experiences for standard systems "rarely have to worry about questions of the following sort:

- When I address a system, how does it know I am addressing it?
- When I ask a system to do something how do I know it is attending?
- When I issue a command (such as save, execute or delete), how does the system know what it relates to?
- How do I know the system understands my command and is correctly executing my intended action?
- How do I recover from mistakes?"

All of these questions, of course, come into play in the context of everyware. They go directly to the heart of the difference between ubiquitous systems and the digital artifacts we're used to. What they tell us is that everyware is not something you sit down in front of, intent on engaging. It's neither something that is easily contained in a session of use, nor an environment in which blunders and missteps can simply be Ctrl-Z'ed away.

What it *is* is a radically new situation that will require the development over time of a doctrine and a body of standards and conventions—starting with the interfaces through which we address it.

Thesis 10

Everyware necessitates a new set of human interface modes.

One of the most obvious ways in which everyware diverges from the PC case is its requirement for input modalities beyond the standard keyboard and screen, trackball, touchpad, and mouse.

With functionality distributed throughout the environment, embedded in objects and contexts far removed from anything you could (or would want to) graft a keyboard onto, the familiar ways of interacting with computers don't make much sense. So right away we have to devise new human interfaces, new ways for people to communicate their needs and desires to the computational systems around them.

Some progress has already been made in this direction, ingenious measures that have sprouted up in response both to the diminutive form factor of current-generation devices and the go-everywhere style of use they enable. Contemporary phones, PDAs, and music players offer a profusion of new interface elements adapted to their context: scroll wheels, voice dialing, stylus-based input, and predictive text-entry systems that, at least in theory, allow users of phone keypads to approximate the speed of typing on a full keyboard.

But as anyone who has spent even a little time with them knows, none of them is entirely satisfactory. At most, they are suggestive of the full range of interventions everyware will require.

One set of possibilities is suggested by the field known as "tangible media" at the MIT Media Lab, and "physical computing" to those researching it at NYU's Interactive Telecommunications Program. The field contemplates bridging the worlds of things and information, atoms and bits: Physical interface elements are manipulated to perform operations on associated data. Such *haptic* interfaces invoke the senses of both touch and proprioception—what you feel through the skin, that is, and the sensorimotor awareness you maintain of the position and movement of your body.

In a small way, using a mouse is physical computing, in that moving an object out in the world affects things that happen on screen. The ease and simplicity most users experience in mousing, after an exceedingly brief period of adaptation upon first use, relies on the subtle consciousness of cursor location that the user retains, perceived solely through the positioning of the wrist joint and fingers. It isn't too far a leap from noticing this to wondering whether this faculty might not be brought directly to bear on the world.

An example of a tangible interface in practice is the "media table" in the lobby of New York's Asia Society, a collaboration between Small Design Firm and media designer Andrew Davies. At first glance, the table appears to be little more than a comfortable place to sit and rest, a sumptuously smooth ovoid onto which two maps of the Asian landmass happen to be projected, each facing a seated user. But spend a few minutes playing with it—as its design clearly invites you to—and you realize that the table is actually a sophisticated interface to the Asia Society's online informational resources.

Off to the table's side, six pucks, smoothly rounded like river stones, nestle snugly in declivities designed specifically for them. Pick one up, feel its comfortable heft, and you see that it bears lettering around its rim: "food," or "news headlines," or "country profiles." And although it's sufficiently obvious from the context that the stones "want" you to place them over the map display, a friendly introduction gives you permission to do just that.

When you do, the map zooms in on the country you've chosen and offers a response to your selection. Holding the "news headlines" stone over Singapore, for example, calls up a live Web feed from the *Straits Times*, while holding "food" over Thailand takes you to recipes for Tom Yum

Kung and Masaman Curry. You can easily spend fifteen minutes happily swapping stones, watching the display smoothly glide in and out, and learning a little bit about Asia as you're doing so.

As the media table suggests, such tangible interfaces are ideal for places where conventional methods would be practically or aesthetically inappropriate, or where the audience might be intimidated by them or uncomfortable in using them. The production values of the lobby are decidedly high, with sumptuous fixtures that include a million-dollar staircase; the Asia Society had already decided that a drab, standard-issue Web kiosk simply wouldn't do. So part of Small Design's reasoning was aesthetic: it wanted to suggest some connection, however fleeting, to the famous garden of the Ryoan-ji temple in Kyoto. If the media table is not precisely Zenlike, it is at the very least a genuine pleasure to touch and use.

But Small also knew that the Asia Society's audience skewed elderly and wanted to provide visitors who might have been unfamiliar with pull-down menus a more intuitive way to access all of the information contained in a complex decision tree of options. Finally, with no moving parts, the media table stands up to the demands of a high-traffic setting far better than a standard keyboard and trackball would have.

Though the Asia Society media table is particularly well-executed in every aspect of its physical and interaction design, the presentation at its heart is still a fairly conventional Web site. More radical tangible interfaces present the possibility of entirely new relationships between atoms and bits.

Jun Rekimoto's innovative DataTiles project, developed at Sony Computer Science Laboratories (CSL), provides the user with a vocabulary of interactions that can be combined in a wide variety of engaging ways—a hybrid language that blends physical cues with visual behaviors. Each DataTile, a transparent pane of acrylic about 10 centimeters on a side, is actually a modular interface element with an embedded RFID tag. Place it on the display and its behaviors change depending on what other tiles it has been associated with. Some are relatively straightforward applications: Weather, Video, and Paint tiles are exactly what they sound like. Playing a Portal tile opens up a hole in space, a linkage to some person, place or object in the real world—a webcam image of a conference room, or the status of a remote printer. Some Portals come with an appealing twist: the Whiteboard module not only allows the user to inscribe their thoughts on a remote display board, but also captures what is written there.

Parameter tiles, meanwhile, constrain the behavior of others. The Time-Machine, for example, bears a representation of a scroll wheel; when it is placed next to a video tile, the video can be scrubbed backward and forward. Finally, inter-tile gestures, made with a stylus, allow media objects to be "sent" from one place or application to another.

From the kind of physical interaction behaviors we see in the media table and the DataTiles, it's only a short step to purely gestural ones, like the one so resonantly depicted in the opening moments of Steven Spielberg's 2002 *Minority Report*. Such gestural interfaces have been a continual area of interest in everyware, extending as they do the promise of interactions that are less self-conscious and more truly intuitive. Like physical interfaces, they allow the user to associate muscle memory with the execution of a given task; theoretically, anyway, actions become nearly automatic, and response times tumble toward zero.

With this payoff as incentive, a spectrum of methods have been devised to capture the retinue of expressive things we do with our hands, from the reasonably straightforward to arcane and highly computationally intensive attempts to infer the meaning of user gestures from video. Some of the more practical rely on RFID-instrumented gloves or jewelry to capture gesture; others depend on the body's own inherent capacitance. Startup Tactiva even offers PC users something called TactaPad, a two-handed touchpad that projects representations of the user's hands on the screen, affording a curious kind of immersion in the virtual space of the desktop.

With the pace of real-world development being what it is, this category of interface seems to be on the verge of widespread adoption. Nevertheless, many complications and pitfalls remain for the unwary.

For example, at a recent convention of cartographers, the technology research group Applied Minds demonstrated a gestural interface to geographic information systems. To zoom in on the map, you place your hands on the map surface at the desired spot and simply spread them apart. It's an appealing representation: immediately recognizable and memorable, intuitive, transparent. It makes sense. Once you've done it, you'll never forget it.

Or so Applied Minds would have you believe. If only gesture were this simple! The association that Applied Minds suggests between a gesture of spreading one's hands and zooming in to a map surface is culturally specific, as arbitrary as any other. Why should spreading not zoom out instead? It's just as defensibly natural, just as "intuitive" a signifier of moving outward as inward. For that matter, many a joke has turned on the fact that certain everyday gestures, utterly unremarkable in one culture—the thumbs-up, the peace sign, the "OK" sign—are vile obscenities in another.

What matters, of course, is not that one particular system may do something idiosyncratically: Anything simple can probably be memorized and associated with a given task with a minimum of effort. The problem emerges when the different systems one is exposed to do things different ways: when the map at home zooms *in* if you spread your hands, but the map in your car zooms *out*.

The final category of new interfaces in everyware concerns something still less tangible than gesture: interactions that use the audio channel. This includes voice-recognition input, machine-synthesized speech output, and the use of "earcons," or auditory icons.

The latter, recognizable tones associated with system events assume new importance in everyware, although they're also employed in the desktop setting. (Both Mac OS and Windows machines can play earcons—on emptying the Trash, for example.) They potentially serve to address one of the concerns raised by the Bellotti paper previously referenced: Used judiciously, they can function as subtle indicators that a system has received, and is properly acting on, some input.

Spoken notifications, too, are useful, in situations where the user's attention is diverted by events in their visual field or by the other tasks that he or she is engaged in: Callers and visitors can be announced by name, emergent conditions can be specified, and highly complex information can be conveyed at arbitrary length and precision.

But of all audio-channel measures, it is voice-recognition that is most obviously called upon in constructing a computing that is supposed to be invisible but everywhere. Voices can, of course, be associated with specific people, and this can be highly useful in providing for differential permissioning—liquor cabinets that unlock only in response to spoken commands issued by adults in the household, journals that refuse access to any but their owners. Speech, too, carries clear cues as to the speaker's emotional state; A household system might react to these alongside whatever content is actually expressed—yes, the volume can be turned down in response to your command, but should the timbre of your voice indicate that stress and not loudness is the real issue, maybe the ambient lighting is softened as well.

We shouldn't lose sight of just how profound a proposition voice-recognition represents when it is coupled to effectors deployed in the wider environment. For the first time, the greater mass of humanity can be provided with a practical mechanism by which their "perlocutionary" utterances—speech acts intended to bring about a given state—can change the shape and texture of reality.

Whatever else comes of this, though, computing equipped with tangible, gestural, and audio-channel interfaces is set free to inhabit a far larger number and variety of places in the world than can be provided for by conventional methods.

Thesis 11

Everyware appears not merely in more places than personal computing does, but in more different kinds of places, at a greater variety of scales.

In principle, at least as far as some of the more enthusiastic proponents of ubicomp are concerned, few human places exist that could not be usefully augmented by networked information processing.

Whether or not we happen to agree with this proposition ourselves, we should consider it likely that over the next few years we'll see computing appear in a very great number of places (and kinds of places) previously inaccessible to it. What would this mean in practice?

Some classic sites for the more traditional sort of personal computing are offices, libraries, dorm rooms, dens, and classrooms. (If we want to be generous, we might include static informational kiosks.)

When people started using wireless-equipped laptops, this domain expanded to include coffee houses, transit lounges, airliner seats, hotel rooms, airport concourses—basically anywhere it would be socially acceptable to sit and balance a five-pound machine on your knees, should it come to that.

The advent of a mobile computing based on smartphones and wireless PDAs opened things up still further, both technically and interpersonally. On top of the kinds of places where laptops are typically used, we can spot people happily tapping away at their mobile devices on, in, and around sidewalks, cars, waiting rooms, supermarkets, bus stops, civic plazas, commuter trains.

But extending this consideration to include ubiquitous systems is almost like dividing by zero. How do you begin to discuss the "place" of computing that subsumes all of the above situations, but also invests processing power in refrigerators, elevators, closets, toilets, pens, tollbooths, eyeglasses, utility conduits, architectural surfaces, pets, sneakers, subway turnstiles, handbags, HVAC equipment, coffee mugs, credit cards, and many other things?

The expansion not merely in the number of different places where computing can be engaged, but in the range of scales involved, is staggering. Let's look at some of them in terms of specific projects and see how everyware manifests in the world in ways and in places previous apparitions of computing could not.

Thesis 12

Everyware acts at the scale of the body.

Of all the new frontiers opening up for computation, perhaps the most startling is that of the human body. As both a rich source of information in itself and the vehicle by which we experience the world, it was probably inevitable that sooner or later somebody would think to reconsider it as just another kind of networked resource.

The motivations for wanting to do so are many: to leverage the body as a platform for mobile services; to register its position in space and time; to garner information that can be used to tailor the provision of other local services, like environmental controls; and to gain accurate and timely knowledge of the living body, in all the occult complexity of its inner workings.

It's strange, after all, to live in our bodies for as long as we do, to know them about as intimately as anything ever can be known, and to still have so little idea about how they work. The opacity of our relationship with our physical selves is particularly frustrating given that our bodies are constantly signaling their status beneath the threshold of awareness, beyond our ability to control them. In every moment of our lives, the rhythm of the heartbeat, the chemistry of the blood, even the electrical conductivity of the skin are changing in response to evolving physical, situational, and emotional environment.

If you were somehow able to capture and interpret these signals, though, all manner of good could come from it. Bacterial and viral infections could be detected and treated, as might nutritional shortfalls or imbalances. Doctors could easily verify their patients' compliance with a prescribed regimen of pharmaceutical treatment or prophylaxis; a wide variety of otherwise dangerous conditions, caught early enough, might yield to timely intervention.

The information is there; all that remains is to collect it. Ideally, this means getting a data-gathering device that does not call undue attention to itself into intimate proximity with the body, over reasonably long stretches of time. A Pittsburgh-based startup called BodyMedia has done just that, designing a suite of soft sensors that operate at the body's surface.

Their SenseWear Patch prototype resembles a sexy, high-tech Band-Aid. Peel the paper off its adhesive backing and seat it on your arm, and its sensors detect the radiant heat of a living organism, switching it on. Once activated, the unit undertakes the production of what BodyMedia calls a "physiological documentary of your body," a real-time collection of data about heart rate, skin temperature, galvanic skin response, and so on, encrypted and streamed to a base station.

Other networked biosensors operate further away from the body. The current state of the art in such technology has to be regarded as Matsushita Electric's prototype Kenko Toware, an instrumented toilet capable of testing the urine for sugar concentration, as well as registering a user's pulse, blood pressure, and body fat. In what is almost certainly a new frontier for biotelemetry, a user can opt to have this data automatically sent to a doctor via the toilet's built-in Internet connection.*

Is such functionality of any real value? While nominally useful in the diagnosis of diabetes, urine testing is regarded as a poor second to blood testing. Most other types of urine-based diagnostics are complicated by the necessity of acquiring an uncontaminated "clean catch," Nevertheless, the significance of Kenko Toware is clear: From now on, even your bodily waste will be parsed, its hidden truths deciphered, and its import considered in the context of other available information.

One can only hope that such communications would be heavily encrypted.

What of that unfolding just the other side of the skin? Without leaving the scale of the body, we encounter a whole range of technical interventions less concerned with the body as process or oracle than with its possibilities as a convenient platform—one that follows us everywhere we go. These have generally been subsumed under the rubric of "wearable computing."

Early experiments in wearability focused on the needs of highly mobile workers—primarily couriers, logistics personnel, law enforcement officers, and other first responders—whose jobs relied on timely access to situational information yet required that they keep their hands free for other tasks. A series of successful academic studies in the 1980s and 1990s, including those at the MIT Media Lab, ETH Zürich, and the Universities of Bristol and Oregon, demonstrated that deploying informatic systems on the body was at least technically feasible.

They were less convincing in establishing that anything of the sort would ever be acceptable in daily life. Researchers sprouting head-up "augmented reality" reticules, the lumpy protuberances of prototype "personal servers," and the broadband cabling to tie it all together may have proven that the concept of wearable computing was valid, but they invariably looked like extras from low-budget cyberpunk films—or refugees from Fetish Night at the anime festival.

University of Toronto professor Steve Mann has easily trumped anyone else's efforts in this regard, willingly exploring full-time life as a cyborg over the course of several years (and still doing so, as of this writing). Mann attempted to negotiate modern life gamely festooned with all manner of devices, including an "eyetap" that provided for the "continuous passive capture, recording, retrieval, and sharing" of anything that happened to pass through his field of vision.

It was difficult to imagine more than a very few people ever submitting to the awkwardness of all this, let alone the bother that went along with being a constant focus of attention; Mann himself was the subject of a notorious incident at the U.S.-Canada border, soon after the September

11th attacks, in which his mediating devices were forcibly removed by immigration authorities.*

But happily for all concerned, the hardware involved in wearable computing has become markedly smaller, lighter, and cheaper. As ordinary people grew more comfortable with digital technology, and researchers developed a little finesse in applying it to the body, it became clear that "wearable computing" need not conjure visions of cyberdork accessories like head-up displays. One obvious solution, once it became practical, was to diffuse networked functionality into something people are already in the habit of carrying on their person at most times: clothing.

In 1999 Philips Electronics published a glossy volume called *New Nomads*, featuring a whole collection of sleek and highly stylish fashions whose utility was amplified by onboard intelligence. While the work was speculative—all the pieces on display were, sadly, nonfunctional mockups and design studies—there was nothing in them that would have looked out of place on the sidewalks or ski slopes of the real world. Philips managed to demonstrate that wearable computing was not merely feasible, but potentially sexy.

Nor did the real world waste much time in catching up. Burton released an iPod-compatible snowboarding jacket called Amp in 2003, with narrow-gauge wiring threaded down the sleeves to a wrist-mounted control panel; by winter 2004-2005, Burton and Motorola were offering a Bluetooth-equipped suite of jacket and beanie that kept snowboarders wirelessly coupled to their phones and music players. The adidas_1 sneaker did still more with embedded processors, using sensors and actuators to adjust the shoe's profile in real time, in response to a runner's biomechanics.

Beyond the things you can already buy, hundreds of student projects have explored the possibilities of sensors light and flexible enough to

---

*This sudden deprivation of the massive input he had become accustomed to was apparently a harrowing experience for Mann. He described it as one of deep disorientation and nausea.

be woven into clothing, typified by Richard Etter and Diana Grathwohl's AwareCuffs—sleeves that sense the digital environment and respond to the presence of an open Wi-Fi network. Given how often the ideas animating such projects have turned up in commercial products just a few years (or even months) later, we can expect the imminent appearance of a constellation of wearables.

And while none of these products and projects are as total as the digital exoskeleton Steve Mann envisioned, maybe they don't have to be. For all his personal bravery in pioneering wearable computing, Mann's vision was the product of a pre-Web, pre-cellular era in which computational resources were a lot scarcer than they are now. When more such resources are deployed in the world, we probably have to carry fewer of them around with us.

So what's the next step? After decades of habituation due to the wristwatch, the outer surface of the forearm is by now a "natural" and intuitive place to put readouts and controls. Meanwhile, with the generous expanse it offers, the torso offers wireless communication devices enough space for a particularly powerful and receptive antenna; a prototype from the U.S. Army's Natick Soldier Center integrates such an antenna into a vest that also provides a (near-literal) backbone for warfighter electronics, optics, and sensor suites. (The Army, at least, is prepared to attest to the safety of such antennae for its personnel, but I'm less certain that anyone not subject to military law would be so sanguine about wearing one all day.)

We'll also see garments with embedded circuitry allowing them to change their physical characteristics in response to external signals. The North Face's MET5 jacket takes perhaps the simplest approach, offering the wearer a controller for the grid of microscopic conductive fibers that carry heat through the garment. But more than one high-profile consumer fashion brand is currently developing clothing whose fibers actually alter their loft, and therefore their insulation profile, when signaled. When coupled to a household management system, this gives us shirts and pants that get more or less insulating, warmer or cooler, depending on the momentary temperature in the room.

Finally, there are a number of products in development that treat the clothed body as a display surface, the garment itself as a site of mediation. The U.S. Army, again, is experimenting with electro-optical camouflage for its next-generation battle dress, which suggests some interesting possibilities for clothing, from animated logos to "prints" that can be updated with the passing seasons. (Real-world approximations of the identity-dissimulating "scramble suits," so memorably imagined by Philip K. Dick in his 1972 *A Scanner Darkly,* are another potential byproduct.)

Considered in isolation, these projects—from toilet to eyetap, from "body area network" to running shoe—are clearly of varying degrees of interest, practicality and utility. But in the end, everything connects. Taken together, they present a clear picture of where we're headed: a world in which the body has been decisively reimagined as a site of networked computation.

Thesis 13

Everyware acts at the scale of the room.

If even the body is subject to colonization by ubiquitous computing, the same is certainly true of the places we spend most of our time in and relate to most readily: architectural spaces of room scale.

As we've seen, most of the early experiments in ubicomp focused on the office environment, and supported the activities that people typically do there. But many aspects of these investigations were applicable to other kinds of spaces and pursuits as well, with processing deployed in features that most rooms have in common: walls, doorways, furniture, and floors.

If you want to provide services to people as they roam freely through a space, it's quite important to know exactly where they are and get some idea of what they might be doing. If their identities have not already been mediated by some other mechanism, it's also useful to be able to differentiate between them. So one strong current of development has concerned the floor beneath our feet, quite literally the perfect platform for sensors able to relay such information.

As far back as 1997, the Olivetti and Oracle Research Lab at the University of Cambridge had developed a prototype Active Floor, which monitored both weight distribution and the time variation of loads. Georgia Tech's Smart Floor followed, improving on Active Floor not least by its attempt to identify users by their "footfall signature," while the University of Florida's Gator Tech Smart House uses flooring throughout with impact sensors capable of detecting falls and reporting them to emergency services.

Two current strains of thinking about smart flooring are represented by very different projects announced within the last year. On one hand, we have NTT DoCoMo's CarpetLAN prototype, which uses weak electrical fields to afford both wireless networking and positioning accurate down to about one meter of resolution. CarpetLAN bears all the marks of a highly sophisticated effort to understand what kinds of functionality can be practically subsumed in a floor.

And then there is inventor Leo Fernekes' Sensacell capacitive sensor grid system, developed in collaboration with architect Joakim Hannerz. It has to be said that Sensacell is not the world's most versatile system. It relies on changes in capacitance to detect presence and location and can therefore pick up conductive objects like the human body, but that's about it. Sensacell returns no load information, offers no way to differentiate between individuals, and certainly isn't designed to establish connections with mobile devices. It's not even necessarily fine-grained enough to distinguish between your transit of a space and the midnight errands of the family cat. And given that its presentation to date has focused on output in the (admittedly quite pretty) form of banks of embedded LEDs, Sensacell seems destined for applications in a relatively narrow swath of high-concept bars, lounges, and retail spaces.

But Sensacell has three big advantages over its predecessors: It's modular, it comes in sizes that conform to the square-foot grid actually used by contractors, and it is commercially available right now. What's more, the luminous cells can be integrated into vertical surfaces, even furniture, and their stream of output data can be jacked into just about any garden-variety PC. The pricing is on the high side, but not absurdly so, and will surely fall in the event of any large-scale production. For all of these reasons, Sensacell is accessible, within reach of the kind of tinkering ubihackers who may be key to the wider spread of everyware.

In addition to flooring, instrumented doorways have also begun to appear. Knowledge of door status can be very useful in context-aware applications—whether an office door is open or closed can imply something about the relative intensity with which the occupant is engaged in a task, while a change in state is generally a marker that a user is transitioning between one activity and another. But door sensors can also be used simply to count how many people enter or leave a given room. (Fire inspectors might want to take note.) California startup InCom's recent pilot program InClass aimed to cut down on teacher administrative time by doing just this, producing a tally of classroom attendance as students wearing RFID-equipped nametags passed beneath a transom-mounted reader.*

If the doorway produces both headcounts and inferences about behavior, and the floor is occasionally called upon to be everything from impact detector to transmission medium, walls have it relatively easy. Most ubiquitous projects to date have treated the wall first and foremost as a large-scale display surface, with its use as a communication hub following from this.

This, of course, conforms to a venerable tradition in science fiction, but such ultraflat, ultrawide screens are now on the verge of practical reality. Motorola's Physical Science Research Laboratory recently presented sections of a prototype carbon nanotube screen 160 cm across diagonally by a single centimeter thick. If either Motorola or its competitors manage to produce nanotube displays at commercial scale, truly wall-spanning displays cannot be far off, although they're still probably years and not months away.

For some interested parties, this may seem like a long time to wait, given the wallscreen's centrality to their visions of the "digital home." In the more elaborate of such schemes, the wall becomes some combination of home theater, videophone, whiteboard, and family scratchpad—a site where downloaded media objects are delivered for consumption, a communication medium in its own right, and the place where other networked devices in the home are managed.

You can already buy appliances ostensibly designed with such distributed control in mind: the first generation of Internet-capable domestic appliances, typified by LG's suite of refrigerator, air conditioner, microwave, and washing machine.

---

*Parents objected to the program on privacy concerns, and the system was withdrawn from operation after less than a month.

Whatever their merits as appliances, however, they completely fail to capitalize on their nature as networked devices capable of communicating with other networked devices, which tends to rule out the more interesting sorts of interaction that might otherwise be envisioned. Users address LG's appliances one by one, via a superficially modified but otherwise entirely conventional Windows interface; the advertised functionality is limited to use cases that must have struck even the marketing department as forced. The webcam-equipped refrigerator, for example, lets family members send each other video memos, while the air conditioner offers new patterns of airflow for download, presumably as one would download polyphonic ring tones. The "Internet" microwave is even worse, forcing a user to connect an external PC to the Web to download recipes.

True utility in the digital room awaits a recognition that the networked whole is distinctly more than the sum of its parts. In contrast with such piecemeal conceptions, there have been others that approached the ubiquitous systems operating in a space as a unified whole.

The MIT Tangible Media Group's 1998 prototype ambientROOM was one such pioneering effort. Built into a free-standing Steelcase office cubicle of around fifty square feet, ambientROOM was nothing if not an exercise in holism: The entire space was considered as an interface, using lighting and shadow, sound cues, and even the rippled reflection of light on water to convey activity meaningful to the occupant. The sound of birdsong and rainfall varied in volume with some arbitrary quantity set by a user—both the "value of a stock portfolio" and the "number of unread e-mail messages" were proposed at the time*—while "active wallpaper" took on new qualities in reaction to the absence or presence of people in a nearby conference room.

---

*Conveying the quantity of unread e-mail is apparently an eternal goal of such systems, while explicitly calling out one's stock portfolio as something to be tracked by the minute seems to have been an artifact of the go-go, day-trading era in which ambientROOM was designed.

Projects like ambientROOM begin to suggest how systems made up of media hubs, wall-screens, networked refrigerators, and all the other appurtenances of room-scale everyware might work when designed in recognition of the person at their heart.

Some of the first to get a taste of this in real life have been high-margin frequent travelers. Since mid-2005, rooms at the Mandarin Oriental in New York have loaded preference files maintained on a central server when the hotel's best customers check in, customizing settings from the shades to the thermostat, lining up entertainment options, and loading frequently dialed numbers into the phone.* "Digital home" solutions that propose to do many of the same things in a domestic setting can be expected to reach the market in the near term, though whether they'll afford experiences of reasonably seamless ubiquity is debatable.

And so we see it cropping up again, here at the scale of the room, this pattern that may by now seem familiar to you: Our discussions of everyware have much less to do with some notional future than they do with a blunt inventory of products already finding their way to market.

---

*As you may have suspected, yes, the hotel does keep track of what you're watching. The potential for embarrassment is real, and is something we'll deal with extensively in Sections 6 and 7.

Thesis 14

Everyware acts at the scale of the building.

In this thesis and the next, which concerns the extension of everyware into public space, we reach scales where the ubiquitous deployment of processing starts to have consequences beyond ones we can easily envision. When we find networked intelligence operating at the scale of whole buildings, it doesn't even necessarily make sense to speak of how the everyware experience diverges from that of personal computing—these are places that people using PCs have rarely if ever been able to reach.

The idea of a building whose program, circulation, and even structure are deeply molded by flows of digital information is nothing new. As a profession, architecture has been assuming that this is going to happen for quite awhile now. The design press of the 1990s was saturated with such visions. Anyone who regularly read *Metropolis* or *wallpaper* or *ID* in those years will likely remember a stream of blobjectified buildings, all nurbly and spliny, with tightly-kerned Helvetica Neue wrapped around the corners to represent "interactive surfaces," and images of Asian women sleekly coutoured in Jil Sander Photoshopped into the foreground to connote generic urban futurity.* But the role played by networked information in such projects mostly seemed to mean some variation on Web-on-the-wall.

For all the lovely renderings, we have yet to see the appearance of buildings structurally modified in any significant way by the provision of real-time, networked information.

Yet since the 1970s, it has been commonplace of commercial architecture and engineering, at least, that information technology allows impressive

---

Architects: I kid. I kid, because I love.

efficiencies to be realized when incorporated in the design of buildings. It is now rare for a new, premium commercial building to break ground without offering some such provision.

Circulation and delivery of services in so-called "smart buildings" can be tuned in real time, in pursuit of some nominal efficiency profile. Instead of stupidly offering an unvarying program of light, heat, and air conditioning, energy management control systems (EMCS) infer appropriate environmental strategies from the time of day and of year, solar gain, and the presence or absence of occupants. And security and custodial staffs are assisted in their duties by the extension of computational awareness throughout the structure. It would be a stretch to call such systems "routine," but only just barely.

Other computationally-enhanced building systems are becoming increasingly common, like Schindler Elevator's Miconic 10, which optimizes load by aggregating passenger groups based on where they're going. Instead of the time-honored principle of pressing an "up" button, and then waiting in a gaggle with all the other upbound passengers, the Miconic 10's clever load-optimization algorithm matches people bound for the same floor with the elevator cab currently offering the shortest wait time. (It's simpler to do than it is to explain.) Schindler claims the elevators make each individual trip 30 percent faster, and also allow a building to handle a proportionally increased flow of visitors.*

When such systems are coupled to the relational, adaptive possibilities offered up by everyware in its other aspects, we start to get into some really interesting territory. The Arch-OS "operating system for architecture," for example, a project of the School of Computing, Communications and

---

*What gets lost, though, in all of this—as with so many digitally "rationalized" processes—is the opportunity for serendipitous interaction that happens when people from different floors share this particular forty-five-second interval of the day. Isn't the whole cherished trope of the "elevator pitch" based around the scenario of a kid from the mailroom finding him- or herself willy-nilly sharing a cab with the CXO types headed for the executive floors?

Electronics at the University of Plymouth, suggests some of the possible directions. As its Web site explains, the project aims to capture the state of a building in real time from inputs including "building energy management systems...the flow of people and social interactions, ambient noise levels and environmental conditions," and return that state to public awareness through a variety of visualizations.

While there's ample reason to believe that such ambient displays of information relating to building systems will become both prevalent and useful, most of the Arch-OS projects to date lean toward the artistic. While it sounds fascinating, for example, it's unclear from the project's documentation whether the "psychometric architecture" project—the recording of activity in a building throughout the day, for playback on its outer envelope at night—was ever attempted. The generative soundscapes and abstract visualizations on hand do seem to mesh well, though, with other recent efforts to equip the outer surfaces of a building with interactive media.

Consider dECOi's 2003 Aegis Hyposurface, a continuously-transformable membrane that allows digital input—whether from microphone, keyboard, or motion sensor—to be physically rendered on the surface itself, showing up as symbols, shapes, and other deformations. Its creators call Aegis "a giant sketchpad for a new age," and while its complexity has kept it from being produced as anything beyond a prototype, it at least was explicitly designed to respond to the kind of inputs Arch-OS produces.

Meanwhile, similar systems, which have actually been deployed commercially, fail to quite close the loop. UNStudio's recent digital facade for Seoul's high-end Galleria department store, developed in association with Arup Engineering and lighting designer Rogier van der Heide, is one such project. The architects wrapped a matrix of LED-illuminated disks around what used to be a drab concrete box, turning the whole surface into a field of ever-renewing data and color. It's a success—it currently bathes the Apgujeong district with gorgeous washes of light nightly—and yet the images flowing across the surface seem to cry out for some generative connection to the inner life of the building.

But already a vanguard few are wrestling with challenges beyond the mere display of information, exploring the new architectural morphologies that become possible when computation is everywhere in the structure itself. Los Angeles–based architect Peter Testa has designed a prototype building called the Carbon Tower: an all-composite, forty-story high-rise knit, braided and woven from carbon fiber.

Unlike conventional architecture, the Carbon Tower dispenses with all internal bracing, able to do so not merely because of the mechanical properties of its textile exoskeleton, but due to the way that exoskeleton is managed digitally. As Testa envisions it, the Carbon Tower exhibits "active lateral bracing": sensors and actuators embedded in its structural fiber cinch the building's outer skin in response to wind load and other dynamic forces.

And if building morphology can be tuned in response to environmental inputs, who's to say that those inputs should be limited to the weather? Arch-OS-style polling of foot traffic and social interactions, coupled to output in the form of structural changes can take us in some genuinely novel directions. Something resembling fondly remembered and much-beloved Archigram projects of the 1960s such as Instant City, Tuned Suburb, and the Control and Choice Dwelling may finally be realized—or so fans of the visionary collective can hope. When compared to the inert structures we now inhabit, everyware-age architecture—for better or worse—will be almost certainly be weirder.

Thesis 15

Everyware acts at the scale of the street and of public space in general.

At present, the most often-pursued applications of everyware at scales beyond the individual building concern wayfinding: knowing where in the world you are and how to get where you're going.

We've become familiar with the idea that dashboard navigation displays using the Global Positioning System (GPS) will help us figure these things out. But GPS is a line-of-sight system—you need to be visible to at least three satellites currently above the horizon in order for it to triangulate your position—so it doesn't work indoors, in tunnels, or in places where there's lots of built-up density. This makes GPS a fairly poor way of finding your way around places like Manhattan, although it seems to work satisfactorily in lower-density conurbations like Tokyo.

Other systems that might help us find our way around the city have their own problems. Schemes that depend on tracking your various personal devices by using the local cellular network can't offer sufficient precision to really be useful as a stand-alone guide. And while the kinds of sensor grids we've discussed in the context of indoor spaces can be accurate to sub-meter tolerances, it would clearly be wildly impractical to deploy them at the scale of a whole city.

But what if the city itself could help you find your way? In 1971, in a landmark study entitled *The Image Of The City*, MIT professor and urbanist Kevin Lynch explored a quality of the city he called "legibility." How do people read a city, in other words? What sorts of features support their attempts to figure out where they are, which paths connect them to a given destination, and how best to actually go about getting there?

Lynch identified a few systems that have historically helped us find our way in the city: signage, of course, but also explicit maps, even street numbering conventions. Such systems function best in a city that itself offers distinctly characterized districts, clearly identifiable paths between them, and above all, the kind of highly visible landmarks that allow people to orient themselves from multiple vantage points, such as Manhattan's Empire State Building, Seoul's Namsan Tower, and Berlin's Fernsehturm. Other kinds of landmarks play a role, too: prominent, easy-to-specify places—the clock in Grand Central Station—where arrivals are readily visible to one another.

All of these features are now subject to computational enhancement. Street furniture such as lamp posts, signage, even manhole covers can provide the urban sojourner with smart waypoints; Tokyo's Shinjuku ward is currently tagging some 10,000 lamp posts with RFID panels that give visitors information on nearby public toilets, subway entrances, and other accommodations.

Meanwhile, maps themselves can offer dynamic, real-time information on position and direction, just as their automotive equivalents do. At Lancaster University, in the UK, just such a prototype public navigation system—dubbed GAUDI, for "grid of autonomous displays"—helps visitors find their way around campus, using adaptive displays as directional signs.

The system's initial release is intended for use as temporary signage for events—lectures, academic conferences, concerts, and the like. Upon being switched on, each portable GAUDI panel queries the navigational server for its current location. It then displays the name and direction of, and approximate distance to, the selected destination. Moving a GAUDI display from one place to another automatically updates it; an arrow that points left to the destination will reverse when placed on the opposite wall.

Nor is GAUDI limited to a selection of fixed campus landmarks. It can direct visitors to that wide variety of campus events that are regular but subject to frequent changes in location—a professor's office hours, or a meeting that has outgrown the auditorium in which it was originally scheduled.

It's easy to see how something like GAUDI, suitably ruggedized and secured, could transform the experience of citing, especially when combined with other locational and directional indicators carried on the body or integrated into clothing. Taken together, they would render the urban domain legible in a way Kevin Lynch could not have imagined in 1970. In such a place, locations self-identify, notices of congestion immediately generate alternative paths to the destination, and services announce themselves. (Anyone who's ever spent the day on foot in one of Earth's great cities will appreciate the prospect of knowing where the nearest public restroom is, even at what time it was last cleaned.)

Information architect Peter Morville calls such interventions in the city "wayfinding 2.0"—an aspect of the emerging informational milieu he thinks of as "ambient findability," in which a combination of pervasive devices, the social application of semantic metadata, and self-identifying objects renders the built environment (and many other things besides) effectively transparent to inquiry.

But as we shall see in some detail, everyware also functions as an extension of power into public space, whether that space be streetscape, commons, station, or stadium—conditioning it, determining who can be there and what services are available to each of them. More deeply still, there are ways in which the deployment of a robust everyware will connect these places with others previously regarded as private. Our very notions of what counts as "public" cannot help but be changed in the aftermath.

Thesis 16

**Everyware can be engaged inadvertently,
unknowingly, or even unwillingly.**

I hope it's obvious by now that one of the most significant ways in which everyware diverges from our experience of personal computing is that in all of the scenarios we've been exploring, it can be engaged even in the absence of an active, conscious decision to do so.

There are at least three modes in which this lack of agency becomes relevant. The first is the situation of inadvertency: *I didn't mean to* engage this system. I didn't mean to broadcast my current location to anybody who asks for it. I meant to do something else—perhaps set it such that only my friends and family could find me—and I've forgotten the command that would limit this function or disable it entirely.

There's also the case where everyware is invoked unknowingly: *I wasn't aware* of this system's extent, domain of operation, capabilities, or ownership. I had no idea that this store tracked my movements through it and would mail me coupons for products I stood next to for more than ten seconds but didn't purchase. I didn't know that this toilet would test my urine for the breakdown products of opiates and communicate its findings to my doctor, my insurers, or law-enforcement personnel. (The consequences of unknowing engagement also affect children, the developmentally disabled, the mentally ill, and others who would be unable to grasp a ubiquitous system's region of influence and their exposure to same.)

Finally, there is the case where the user is unwilling: *I don't want to* be exposed to this system, but I have been compelled by simple expedience, by social convention, by exhaustion, by force of regulation or law to accept such an exposure. I don't want to wear an RFID nametag, but my job requires me to. I'd rather not have my precise weight be a matter of public record, but the only way from my desk to the bathroom has load sensors built into the flooring. I know that the bus will query my ID and maybe I don't want that, but the hour is late; despite my disinclination, I don't have the energy to find an alternative.

How different this is from most of the informational systems we're accustomed to, which, for the most part, require conscious action even if we are to betray ourselves. The passive nature of our exposure to the networked sensor grids and other methods of data collection implied by everyware implicates us whether we know it or not, want it or not. In such a regime, information is constantly being gathered and acted upon, sensed and responded to, archived and retrieved, in ways more subtle than those that function at present.

But inadvertent, unknowing, or unwilling engagement of everyware means more than a simple disinclination to be sensed or assayed. There is also our exposure to the output of ubiquitous systems, to the regular-ized, normalized, optimized courses of action that so often result from the algorithmic pursuit of some nominal profile. Maybe we'd prefer the room to remain refreshingly crisp overnight, not "comfortably" warm; maybe we actually get a charge from the sensation of fighting upstream against the great surge of commuters emerging from the station at 8:45 each morning. Or maybe we simply want to revel in the freedom to choose such things, however uncomfortable, rather than have the choices made for us.

Right now, these aspects of our environment are freely variable, not con-nected to anything else except in the most tenuous and existential way. Where networked information-processing systems are installed, this is no longer necessarily the case.

Thesis 17

The overwhelming majority of people experiencing everyware will not be knowledgeable about information technology.

When computing was something that took place behind the walls of corporate data centers and campus Comp Sci labs, its user base was demographically homogeneous. There were simply not that many ways in which a computer user of the mid-1960s could vary: In North America, anyway, we know that they were overwhelmingly male, overwhelmingly white, overwhelmingly between the ages of 18 and, say, 40 at the outside; they were, by definition, highly educated.

So it was entirely reasonable for the designers of computing systems of the time to suppose that their users shared a certain skill set, even a certain outlook. In fact, the homogeneity went still deeper. The intricacies of arcane languages or the command-line interface simply didn't present a problem in the early days of computing, because the discourse was founded on a tacit assumption that every *user* was also a *developer*, a programmer comfortable with the intellectual underpinnings of computer science.

Every stage in the material evolution of computing, though, has undermined this tidy equation, starting with the introduction of time-sharing systems in the mid-1960s. The practical effect of time sharing was to decouple use of the machine from physical and, eventually, cultural proximity. Relatively cheap and robust remote terminals found their ways into niches in which mainframes would never have made sense either economically or practically, from community centers to elementary schools, multiplying those mainframes' reach by the hundredfold.

It was no longer safe to assume that a user was a fungibly clean-cut, by-the-numbers CS major.

The safety of any such assumption was further damaged by the advent of the personal computer, a device which by dint of its relative portability, affordability, and autonomy from regulation gathered grade-schoolers and grandmothers as users. The audience for computing has only gotten larger and more diverse with every reduction in the PC's size, complexity, and price. The apotheosis of this tendency to date is the hand-cranked "$100 laptop" currently being developed by the MIT Media Lab, intended for the hundreds of millions of semiliterate or even nonliterate potential users in the developing world.

But such assumptions will be shattered completely by everyware. How could it be otherwise? Any technology that has been so extensively insinuated into everyday life, at so many scales, in space both public and private, cannot help but implicate the greatest possible number and demographic diversity of users. Only a small minority of them will have any significant degree of competence with information technology (although it's also true that tropes from the technological realm are increasingly finding their way into mass culture). Still more so than the designers of personal computers, smartphones, or PDAs, those devising ubiquitous systems will have to accommodate the relative technical non-sophistication of their enormous user base.

Thesis 18

In many circumstances, we can't really conceive of the human being engaging everyware as a "user."

Traditionally, the word we use to describe the human person engaged in interaction with a technical system is "user": "user-friendly," "user-centered." (More pointedly, and exposing some of the frustration the highly technically competent may experience when dealing with nonspecialists: "luser.")

Despite this precedent, however, the word stumbles and fails in the context of everyware. As a description of someone encountering ubiquitous systems, it's simply not accurate.

At the most basic level, one no more "uses" everyware than one would a book to read or the floor to stand on. For many of the field's originators, the whole point of designing ubiquitous systems was that they would be ambient, peripheral, and *not* focally attended to in the way that something actively "used" must be.

Perhaps more importantly, "user" also fails to reflect the sharply reduced volitionality that is so often bound up with such encounters. We've already seen that everyware is something that may be engaged by the act of stepping into a room, so the word carries along with it the implication of an agency that simply may not exist.

Finally, exactly because of its historical pedigree in the field, the term comes with some baggage we might well prefer to dispense with. As HCI researcher Jonathan Grudin has argued, because "the computer is assumed [and] the user must be specified" even in phrases like "user-centered design," such terminology "retains and reinforces an engineering perspective" inimical to our present concerns.

I think we might be better served by a word that did a better job of evoking the full, nuanced dimensions of what is experienced by someone encountering everyware. The trouble is that most other candidate words succumb to the same trap that ensnares "user." They also elide one or more important aspects of this person's experience.

Of the various alternative terms that might be proposed, there is one that captures two aspects of the everyware case that happen to be in real tension with one another, both of which are necessary to account for: "subject."

On the one hand, a subject is someone with interiority, with his or her own irreducible experience of the world; one *has subjectivity*. But interestingly enough, we also speak of a person without a significant degree of choice in a given matter as being *subject to* something: law, regulation, change. As it turns out, both senses are appropriate in describing the relationship between a human being and the types of systems we're interested in.

But a moment's consideration tells us that "subject" is no good either. To my ears, anyway, it sounds tinny and clinical, a word that cannot help but conjure up visions of lab experiments, comments inscribed on clipboards by white-coated grad students. I frankly cannot imagine it being adopted for this purpose in routine speech, either by professionals in the field or by anyone else.

So we may be stuck with "user" after all, at least for the foreseeable future, no matter how inaccurate it is. Perhaps the best we can hope for is to remain acutely mindful of its limitations.

Thesis 19

Everyware is always situated in a particular context.

Nothing takes place in a vacuum. As former PARC researcher Paul Dourish observes, in his 2001 study *Where the Action Is*, "interaction is intimately connected with the settings in which it occurs." His theory of "embodied interaction" insists that interactions derive their meaning by occurring in real time and real space and, above all, among and between real people.

In Dourish's view, the character and quality of interactions between people and the technical systems they use depend vitally on the fact that both are embedded in the world in specific ways. A video chat is shaped by the fact that I'm sitting in *this* office, in other words, with its particular arrangement of chair, camera, and monitor, and not *that* one; whether a given gesture will seem to be an appropriate mapping to a system command will seem different depending on whether the user is Sicilian or Laotian or Senegalese.

This seems pretty commonsensical, but it's something that by and large we've been able to overlook throughout the PC era. This is because personal computing is something that we've historically conceived of as being largely independent of context.

In turning on your machine, you enter the nonspace of its interface—and that nonspace is identical whether your laptop is sitting primly atop your desk at work or teetering atop your knees on the library steps. Accessing the Web through such interfaces only means that the rabbit hole goes deeper; as William Gibson foresaw in the first few pages of *Neuromancer*, it really is as if each of our boxes is a portal onto a "consensual hallucination" that's always there waiting for us. No wonder technophiles of the early 1990s were so enthusiastic about virtual reality: it seemed like the next logical step in immersion.

By instrumenting the actual world, though, as opposed to immersing a user in an information-space that never was, everyware is something akin to virtual reality turned inside out. So it matters quite a lot when we propose to embed functionality in all the surfaces the world affords us: we find ourselves deposited back in actuality with an almost-audible thump, and things work differently here. If you want to design a system that lets drive-through customers "tap and go" from the comfort of their cars, you had better ensure that the reader is within easy reach of a seated driver; if your building's smart elevator system is supposed to speed visitor throughput, it probably helps to ensure that the panel where people enter their floors isn't situated in a way that produces bottlenecks in the lobby.

Interpersonal interactions are also conditioned by the apparently trivial fact that they take place in real space. Think of all of the subtle, nonverbal cues we rely upon in the course of a multi-party conversation and how awkward it can be when those cues are stripped away, as they are in a conference call.

Some ubiquitous systems have made attempts at restoring these cues to mediated interactions—one of Hiroshi Ishii's earlier projects, for example, called ClearBoard. ClearBoard attempted to "integrate interpersonal space and shared workspace seamlessly"; it was essentially a shared digital whiteboard, with the important wrinkle that the image of a remote collaborator was projected onto it, "behind" what was being drawn on the board itself.

Not only did this allow partners working at a distance from one another to share a real-time workspace, it preserved crucial indicators like "gestures, head movements, eye contact, and gaze direction"—all precisely the sort of little luxuries that do so much to facilitate communication in immediate real space and that are so often lacking in the virtual.

A sensitively designed everyware will take careful note of the qualities our experiences derive from being situated in real space and time. The more we learn, the more we recognize that such cues are more than mere niceties—that they are, in fact, critical to the way we make sense of our interactions with one another.

Thesis 20

Everyware unavoidably invokes the specter of multiplicity.

One word that should bedevil would-be developers of everyware is "multiple," as in multiple systems, overlapping in their zones of influence; multiple inputs to the same system, some of which may conflict with each other; above all, multiple human users, each equipped with multiple devices, acting simultaneously in a given space.

As we've seen, the natural constraints on communication between a device and its human user imposed by a one-to-one interaction model mean that a PC never has to wonder whether I am addressing it, or someone or -thing else in our shared environment. With one application open to input at any given time, it never has to parse a command in an attempt to divine which of a few various possibilities I might be referring to. And conversely, unless some tremendously processor-intensive task has monopolized it for the moment, I never have to wonder whether the system is paying attention to me.

But the same thing can't really be said of everyware. The multiplicity goes both ways, and runs deep.

Perhaps my living room has two entirely separate and distinct voice-activated systems—say, the wallscreen and the actual window—to which a command to "close the window" would be meaningful. How are they to know which window I mean?

Or maybe our building has an environmental control system that accepts input from personal body monitors. It works just fine as long as there's only one person in the room, but what happens when my wife's monitor reports that she's chilly at the same moment that mine thinks the heat should be turned down?

It's not that such situations cannot be resolved. Of course they can be. It's just that designers will have to explicitly anticipate such situations and devise rules to address them—something that gets exponentially harder when wallscreen and window, shirt telemetry and environmental control system, are all made by different parties.

Multiplicity in everyware isn't just a user-experience issue, either. It's a question that goes directly to the management and allocation of computational resources, involving notions of precedence. Given the resources available locally, which of the many running processes present gets served first? What kind of coordinating mechanisms become necessary?

The situation is complicated still further by the fact that system designers cannot reasonably foresee how these multiple elements will behave in practice. Ideally, a pervasive household network should be able to mediate not merely among its own local, organic resources, but whatever transient ones are brought into range as well.

People come and go, after all, with their personal devices right alongside them. They upgrade the firmware those devices run on, or buy new ones, and those all have to work too. Sometimes people lose connectivity in the middle of a transaction; sometimes their devices crash. As Tim Kindberg and Armando Fox put it, in their 2002 paper "System Software for Ubiquitous Computing," "[a]n environment can contain infrastructure components, which are more or less fixed, and *spontaneous* components based on devices that arrive and leave routinely." Whatever infrastructure is proposed to coordinate these activities had better be able to account for all of that.

Kindberg and Fox offer designers a guideline they call the Volatility Principle: "You should design ubicomp systems on the assumption that the set of participating users, hardware and software is highly dynamic and unpredictable. Clear invariants that govern the entire system's execution should exist."

In other words, no matter what kind of hell might be breaking loose otherwise, it helps to have some kind of stable arbitration mechanism. But with so many things happening at once in everyware, the traditional event queue—the method by which a CPU allocates cycles to running processes—just won't do. A group of researchers at Stanford (including Fox) has proposed a replacement better suited to the demands of volatility: the *event heap*.

Without getting into too much detail, the event heap model proposes that coordination between heterogeneous computational processes be handled by a shared abstraction called a "tuple space." An event might be a notification of a change in state, like a wireless tablet coming into the system's range, or a command to perform some operation; any participating device can write an event to the tuple space, read one out, or copy one from it so that the event in question remains available to other processes.

In this model, events expire after a specified elapse of time, so they're responded to either immediately, or (in the event of a default) not at all. This keeps the heap itself from getting clogged up with unattended-to events, and it also prevents a wayward command from being executed so long after its issuance that the user no longer remembers giving it. Providing for such expiry is a canny move; imagine the volume suddenly jumping on your bedside entertainment system in the middle of the night, five hours after you had told it to.

The original Stanford event heap implementation, called iRoom, successfully coordinated activities among several desktop, laptop, and tablet Windows PCs, a Linux server, Palm OS, and Windows CE handheld devices, multiple projectors, and a room lighting controller. In this environment, moving a pointer from an individual handheld to a shared display was easily achieved, while altering a value in a spreadsheet on a PDA updated a 3D model on a machine across the room. Real-world collaborative work was done in iRoom. It was "robust to failure of individual interactors," and it had been running without problems for a year and a half at the time the paper describing it was published.

It wasn't a perfect solution—the designers foresaw potential problems emerging around scalability and latency—but iRoom and the event heap model driving it were an important first response to the challenges of multiplicity that the majority of ubiquitous systems will eventually be forced to confront.

Thesis 21

Everyware recombines practices and technologies in ways that are greater than the sum of their parts.

The hundred-billion-dollar question: do the products and services we've been discussing truly constitute a system, a continuous fabric of computational awareness and response?

Some—including, it must be said, some of the most knowledgeable, prominent, and respected voices in academic ubicomp—would say that they clearly do not. Their viewpoint is that originators such as Mark Weiser never intended "ubiquitous" to mean anything but *locally* ubiquitous: present everywhere "in the woodwork" of a given, bounded place, not literally circumambient in the world. They might argue that it's obtuse, disingenuous, or technically naive to treat artifacts as diverse as a PayPass card, a SenseWear patch, a Sensacell module, a Miconic 10 elevator system, and a GAUDI display as either epiphenomena of a deeper cause or constituents of a coherent larger-scale system.

If I agreed with them, however, I wouldn't have bothered writing this book. All of these artifacts treat of nothing but the same ones and zeroes, and in principle there is no reason why they could not share information with each other. Indeed, in many cases there will be—or will appear to be—very good reasons why the streams of data they produce should be merged with the greater flow. I would go so far as to say that if the capacity exists, it will be leveraged.

To object that a given artifact was not designed with such applications in mind is to miss the point entirely. By reconsidering them all as network resources, everyware brings these systems into a new relationship with each other that is decidedly more than the sum of their parts. In the sections that follow, I will argue that, however discrete such network-capable systems may be at their design and inception, their interface with each other implies a significantly broader domain of action—a skein of numeric mediation that stretches from the contours of each individual human body outward to satellites in orbit.

I will argue, further, that since the technical capacity to fuse them already exists, we *have* to treat these various objects and services as instantiations of something larger—something that was already by 1990 slouching toward Palo Alto to be born; that it simply makes no sense to consider a biometric patch or a directional display in isolation—not when output from the one can furnish the other with input; and that if we're to make sense of the conjoined impact of these technologies, we have to attend to the effects they produce as a coordinated system of articulated parts.

Thesis 22

Everyware is relational.

One of the more significant effects we should prepare for is how fiercely relational our lives will become. In a world saturated with everyware, responses to the actions we take here and now will depend not only on our own past actions, but also on an arbitrarily large number of other inputs gathered from far afield.

At its most basic, all that "relational" means is that values stored in one database can be matched against those from another, to produce a more richly textured high-level picture than either could have done alone. But when the number of available databases on a network becomes very large, the number of kinds of facts they store is diverse, and there are applications able to call on many of them at once, some surprising things start to happen.

Consider the price of your morning cup of coffee. At present, as any businessperson will tell you, retail pricing is one of the black arts of capitalism. As with any other business, a coffee retailer bases its pricing structure on a calculus designed to produce a profit after accounting for all of the various costs involved in production, logistics, marketing, and staffing—and in many cases this calculus is best described as an educated guess.

The calculus is supposed to find a "sweet spot" that balances two concerns that must be brought together to conclude a sale: the minimum the retailer can afford to charge for each cup and still make a profit, and the maximum you're willing to pay for that cup.

Famously, though, there's many a slip 'twixt cup and lip. For one thing, both values are constantly changing—maybe as often as several times a day. The first fluctuates with the commodities market, transportation costs, and changes in wage laws; the second responds to moves made by competitors as well as factors that are far harder to quantify, like your mood or the degree of your craving for caffeine. Nor does any present pricing model account for things like the variation in rent between different retail locations.

There's simply no practical way to capture all of this variability, and so all these factors get averaged out in the formulation of pricing structures. However expertly devised, they're always something akin to a stab in the dark.

But remember the event heap? Remember how it allowed a value entered *here* to affect a process unfolding *over there*? A world with ubiquitous inputs and event-heap-style coordinating mechanisms writ large turns this assumption upside down. Imagine how much more fluid and volatile the price of a tall decaf latte would be if it resulted from an algorithm actually pegged to something like a real-time synopsis of all of the factors impingent upon it—not only those involved in its production, but also whatever other quantifiable considerations influenced your decision to buy it.

Objections that consumers wouldn't stand still for such price volatility are easily countered by arguing that such things matter much less when the customer does not attend to the precise amount of a transaction. This widely happens to be the case already when the point-of-purchase scenario involves credit and debit cards, and it will surely happen more often as the mechanism of payment increasingly dissolves in behavior.

Say the price was a function of the actual cost of the Jet A fuel that flew this lot of beans in from Kona, the momentary salary of the driver who delivered it...and a thousand other elements. Maybe it reflects a loyalty bonus for having bought your morning jolt from the same store on 708 of the last 731 days, or the weather, or even the mass psychology of your particular market at this particular moment. (Derived—who knows?—from the titration of breakdown products of Prozac and Xanax in the municipal sewage stream.)

This is economics under the condition of ambient informatics. As it happens, many of these quantities are already easily recoverable, even without positing sensors in the sewers and RFID tags on every bag and pallet.

They exist, right now, as numeric values in a spreadsheet or a database somewhere. All that is necessary to begin deriving higher-order information from them is for some real-time coordinating mechanism to allow heterogeneous databases, owned by different entities and maintained in different places, to talk to each other over a network. This way of determining price gets asymptotically close to one of the golden assumptions of classical economics, the frictionlessness of information about a commodity. Consumers could be sure of getting something very close to the best price consistent with the seller's reasonable expectation of profit. In this sense, everyware would appear to be late capitalism's Holy Grail.

And where sharing such information was once anathema to business, this is no longer necessarily true. Google and Yahoo! already offer open application programming interfaces (APIs) to valuable properties like Google Maps and the Flickr photo-sharing service, and the practice is spreading; business has grown comfortable sharing even information traditionally held much closer to the vest, like current inventory levels, with partners up and down the supply chain. When mutual benefit has once been scented, connection often follows.

Beyond this point, the abyss of ridiculously granular relational micropayment schemes opens up. Accenture Technology Labs has demo'd a pay-per-use *chair*, for example, which monitors use, charges according to a schedule of prices that fluctuates with demand, and generates a monthly statement. While one hopes this is at least a little tongue-in-cheek, there is nothing that separates it in principle from other everyware-enabled dynamic pricing models that have been proposed—close-to-real-time insurance premiums, for example, based on the actual risk incurred by a client at any given moment.

Relationality has its limits. We know that a change anywhere in a tightly-coupled system ripples and cascades through everything connected to it, under the right (or wrong) circumstances rendering the whole mesh exquisitely vulnerable to disruption. Nevertheless, it's hard to imagine that a world so richly provisioned with sources of information, so interwoven with the means to connect them, would not eventually provoke someone to take maximum advantage of their joining.

Thesis 23

Everyware has profoundly different social implications than previous information-technology paradigms.

By its very nature, a computing so pervasive and so deeply intertwined with everyday life will exert a transformative influence on our relationships with ourselves and with each other.

In fact, wherever it appears in the world, everyware is always already of social consequence. It can hardly be engaged without raising issues of trust, reputation, credibility, status, respect, and the presentation of self.

Take JAPELAS, a recent Tokushima University project that aims to establish the utility of ubiquitous technology in the classroom—in this case, a Japanese-language classroom. One of the complications of learning to speak Japanese involves knowing which of the many levels of politeness is appropriate in a given context, and this is just what JAPELAS sets out to teach.

The system determines the "appropriate" expression by trying to assess the social distance between interlocutors, their relative status, and the overall context of their interaction; it then supplies the student with the chosen expression, in real time.

Context is handled straightforwardly: Is the setting a bar after class, a job interview, or a graduation ceremony? Social distance is also relatively simple to determine—are these students in my class, in another class at the same school, or do they attend a different school altogether? But to gauge social status, JAPELAS assigns a rank to every person in the room, and this ordering is a function of a student's age, position, and affiliations.

The previous paragraph probably won't raise any red flags for Japanese readers. Why should it? All that JAPELAS does is encode into a technical system rules for linguistic expression that are ultimately derived from conventions about social rank that already existed in the culture. Any native speaker of Japanese makes determinations like these a hundred times a day, without ever once thinking about them: a senior outranks a freshman, a TA outranks a student, a tenured professor outranks an adjunct, and a professor at one of the great national universities outranks somebody who teaches at a smaller regional school. It's "natural" and "obvious."

But to me, it makes a difference when distinctions like these are inscribed in the unremitting logic of an information-processing system.* Admittedly, JAPELAS is "just" a teaching tool, and a prototype at that, so maybe it can be forgiven a certain lack of nuance; you'd be drilled with the same rules by just about any human teacher, after all. (I sure was.) It is nevertheless disconcerting to think how easily such discriminations can be hard-coded into something seemingly neutral and unimpeachable and to consider the force they have when uttered by such a source. And where PC-based learning systems also observe such distinctions, they generally do so in their own bounded nonspace, not out here in the world.

Everyware may not always reify social relations with quite the same clunky intensity that JAPELAS does, but it will invariably reflect the assumptions its designers bring to it. Just as with JAPELAS, those assumptions will result in orderings—and those orderings will be manifested pervasively, in everything from whose preferences take precedence while using a

---

*As someone nurtured on notions of egalitarianism, however hazy, the idea that affiliations have rank especially raises my hackles. I don't like the idea that the city I was born in, the school I went to, or the military unit I belonged to peg me as belonging higher (or lower) on the totem pole than anyone else. Certain Britons, Brahmins, and graduates of the Ecole Normale Supérieure may have a slightly easier time accepting the idea.

home-entertainment system to which of the injured supplicants clamoring for the attention of the ER staff gets cared for first.

As if that weren't enough to chew on, there will also be other significant social consequences of everyware. Among other things, the presence of an ambient informatics will severely constrain the presentation of self, even to ourselves.

This is because information that can be called upon at any time and in any place necessarily becomes part of social transactions in a way that it could not when bound to fixed and discrete devices. We already speak of Googling new acquaintances—whether prospective hires or potential lovers—to learn what we can of them. But this is rarely something we do in their presence; it's something we do, rather, when we remember it, back in front of our machine, hours or days after we've actually made the contact.

What happens when the same information is pushed to us in real time, at the very moment we stand face to face with someone else? What happens when we're offered a new richness of facts about a human being—their credit rating, their claimed affinities, the acidity of their sweat—from sources previously inaccessible, especially when those facts are abstracted into high-level visualizations as simple (and decisive) as a check or a cross-mark appearing next to them in the augmented view provided by our glasses?

And above all, what happens when the composite view we are offered of our own selves conflicts with the way we would want those selves to be perceived?

Erving Goffman taught us, way back in 1958, that we are all actors. We all have a collection of masks, in other words, to be swapped out as the exigencies of our transit through life require: one hour stern boss, the next anxious lover. Who can maintain a custody of the self conscious and consistent enough to read as coherent throughout all the input modes everyware offers?

What we're headed for, I'm afraid, is a milieu in which sustaining different masks for all the different roles in our lives will prove to be untenable, if simply because too much information about our previous decisions will follow us around. And while certain futurists have been warning us about this for years, for the most part even they hadn't counted on the emergence of a technology capable of closing the loop between the existence of such information and its actionability in everyday life. For better or worse, everyware is that technology.

We've taken a look, now, at the ways in which everyware will differ from personal computing and seen that many of its implications are quite profound. Given the magnitude of the changes involved, and their disruptive nature, why does this paradigm shift seem so inevitable? Why have I felt so comfortable asserting that this will happen, or is happening, or even, occasionally, has happened? Especially about something that at the moment mostly seems to be manifested in prototypes and proofs of concept? You may recall that I believe the emergence of everyware is overdetermined—and in the next section, we'll get into a good deal of depth as to why I think this is so.

What's driving the emergence of everyware?

Section 2 explored why the transition from personal computing to a technology of ubiquitous networked devices is truly a "paradigm shift." Why does the emergence of such a radical and potentially disruptive technology seem so ineluctable? What are some of the converging trends that support its emergence?

Thesis 24

Everyware, or something very much like it, is effectively inevitable.

We've considered some of the ways the emergence of everyware seems to be overdetermined. There are forces aplenty driving its appearance, from the needs of the elderly infirm in the world's richest societies to those of nonliterate users in the developing world.

There is an argument to be made that the apparent significance of these drivers is illusory—that Weiser and the other prophets of ubiquitous technology were simply wrong about what people would want from computing, and particularly that they underestimated the persistent appeal of the general-purpose desktop machine despite its flaws.

In this view, most of the products or services we've discussed here will come to fruition, but they'll never amount to much more than bits and pieces, an incoherent scatter of incompatible technologies. Meanwhile, for quite some time to come, we'll continue to interact with information technology much as we have for the last decade, using ever more-sophisticated and possibly more-"converged," but essentially conventional, PCs.

In fairness, there's plenty of empirical support for this position. The streamlined "information appliances" Don Norman imagined got their trial in the market and failed; despite flattering notices in magazine articles and the like, I've never actually met someone who owns one of the "ambient devices" supposed to represent the first wave of calm technology for the home. There seems to be little interest in the various "digital home" scenarios, even among the cohort of consumers who could afford such things and have been comparatively enthusiastic about high-end home theater.*

But I don't think this is anything like the whole story. In fact, barring the wholesale collapse of highly technological civilization on Earth, I believe the advent of some fairly robust form of everyware is effectively inevitable, at least in the so-called "First World." So many of the necessary material and intellectual underpinnings are already fully developed, if not actually deployed, that it is very hard to credit scenarios beyond the near term in which ubiquitous computing does not play some role in everyday life. All the necessary pieces of the puzzle are sitting there on the tabletop, waiting for us to pick them up and put them together.

But let's first do away with the idea that I am depending on a lawyerly, not to say Clintonian, parsing of definitions. Proclaiming the inevitability of everyware would be a fatuously empty proposition if all I meant by it was that touchless e-cash transactions would begin to replace credit cards, or that you'll soon be able to answer your phone via your television. I mean to assert, rather, that everyware, the regime of ambient informatics it gives rise to, and the condition of ambient findability they together entrain, will have significant and meaningful impact on the way you live your life and will do so before the first decade of the twenty-first century is out.

This is such a strong claim that I'll devote the remainder of this section to supporting it in sufficient detail that I believe you will be convinced, whatever your feelings at the moment.

---

*A Motorola executive, interviewed in a recent issue of The Economist, asserted the rather patronizing viewpoint that if customers didn't want these conveniences, they'd simply have to be "educated" about their desirability until they did manage to work up the appropriate level of enthusiasm. In other words, "the floggings will continue until morale improves."

Thesis 25

Everyware has already staked a claim on our visual imaginary, which in turn exerts a surprising influence on the development of technology.

Before we turn to more material drivers, we might first want to attend to a surprisingly influential force that does so much to bolster everyware's aura of inevitability, and that is how often we've already seen it.

More so than in many other fields of contemporary technologic endeavor, in everyware pop culture and actual development have found themselves locked in a co-evolutionary spiral. Time and again, the stories we've told in the movies and the pages of novels have gone on to shape the course of real-world invention. These, in their turn, serve as seed-stock for ever more elaborate imaginings, and the cycle continues.

Beyond genre SF, where the eventual hegemony of some kind of ubiquitous computing has long been an article of faith, traces of everyware's arrival have already turned up in literary fiction. David Foster Wallace lightly drops one or two such intimations into his recent short story "Mister Squishy," while Don DeLillo captures the zeitgeist particularly well in his 2003 *Cosmopolis*; the latter's protagonist, a maximally connected trader in currencies, muses that the discrete devices he relies on are "already vestigial...degenerate structures."*

**"Computers will die. They're dying in their present form. They're just about dead as distinct units. A box, a screen, a keyboard. They're melting into the texture of everyday life...even the word 'computer' sounds backward and dumb." But for the punchy cadence, the words could well be Mark Weiser's.*

Despite these surfacings, though, as well as the undeniable cultural impact of some other visions which have similarly never left the printed page—William Gibson's original depiction of cyberspace comes to mind—it's the things we see up on the screen that generally leave the strongest emotional impression on us.

Movies have certainly shaped the conception of ubiquitous artifacts before, from Jun Rekimoto's DataTiles, the design of which was explicitly inspired by HAL 9000's transparent memory modules in *2001: A Space Odyssey*, to a long series of products and services that seem to owe their visual forms entirely to the influence of 1970's *THX 1138*. But for most nonaficionados, everyware's most explicit and memorable claim on the visual imaginary has been the 2002 *Minority Report*.

For *Minority Report*, director Steven Spielberg asked interaction and interface designers from the MIT Media Lab, Microsoft Research, Austin-based Milkshake Media, and elsewhere to imagine for him what digital media might look like in 2045. They responded with a coherent vision binding together: embedded sensor grids, gestural manipulation of data, newspaperlike information appliances, dynamic and richly personalized advertising, and ubiquitous biometric identification, all undergirded by a seamless real-time network. There is no doubt that their vision, interpreted for the screen, helped mold our shared perception of what would be technically possible, likely, or desirable in next-generation computing.

But before that could happen, a little alchemy would be required. With one or two exceptions, the actual prototypes submitted to the *Minority* production are awkward and unconvincing. They look, in fact, like what they are: things designed by engineers, for engineers. It took futurists immersed in the art of visual storytelling to take these notions and turn them into something compelling—and it was the synthesis of all these ideas in the vivid, if scenery-chewing, vignette that opens *Minority Report* that sold it.

True, the same ideas could have been (and of course had been) presented in academic papers and research conferences and gone little remarked upon outside the community of people working in human-computer interaction. But when situated in a conventionally engaging narrative, animated by recognizable stars, and projected onto megaplexed screens with all of the awesome impact of a Hollywood blockbuster, this set of notions about interface immediately leapt from the arcane precincts of academe into the communal imaginary.

This is partly a matter of the tools any film has at its disposal (emotional, evocative, environment-shaping) and partly a simple matter of scale. Unlike, say, the audience for this book, *Minority Report*'s audience was probably not one composed of people inclined to think about such things outside the context of imaginings on screen, at least not in any detail. But over the course of their two hours in the dark, millions of moviegoers absorbed a vivid idea of what might be working its way toward them, a hook on which to hang their own imaginings and expectations. And where a scholarly paper on gestural device interfaces might be read by tens of thousands, at most, the total lifetime audience for such a thing is easily trumped by a blockbuster's on its opening weekend alone.

Closing the circuit, some members of that audience then go on to furnish the world with the things they've seen. The imaginary informs the world—not of 2045, as it turns out, but of 2005: Media Lab alumnus John Underkoffler, designer of the gesture-driven interface in *Report*, was sought out by a group at defense contractor Raytheon, whose members had seen and been impressed by the film. He was eventually hired by Raytheon to develop similar systems for the U.S. military's "net-centric warfare" efforts, including a shared interface called the Common Tactical Blackboard.

Thus is the fantastic reified, made real.

Thesis 26

Something with the properties we see in everyware was foreordained the moment tools and services began to be expressed digitally.

Long before there was an everyware, we simply had tools. Some of them were mechanical in nature, like timepieces and cameras. Others were electric, or electronic, in whole or in part: radios, telephones, televisions. Others still were larger, less mobile, designed to perform a single function: appliances. And together, they comprised a technics of everyday life.

It was, of course, an analog universe. Where these tools gathered information about the world, it was encoded as the state of a continuously variable physical system: so many turns of a toothed wheel, an etched groove of such-and-such depth. And this had its advantages: to this day, there are those who swear by the tone and richness of analog recordings or the images produced by the fall of light on film grain.

In time, though, many of the tools that had been electric, mechanical, or some combination of the two were recast as digital, which is to say that when they encoded information about the world, it was rendered as a discrete, stepped progression of ones and zeroes. This afforded perfect fidelity in reproduction, more efficient transmission, all but cost-free replication. And so the analog Walkman gave way to the digital iPod, the Motorola MicroTAC begat the RAZR, the original Canon Elph became—what else?—the Digital Elph.

None of the analog devices could have communicated with each other—they barely even *related* to one another. What, after all, does a song on cassette have to do with an image burned into film? You could rub them against each other all day and not get anything for your trouble but scratched celluloid, tangled up in ribbons of magnetic tape. What could you have done with either over a telephone, except tell the person on the other end of the line all about the neat songs and pretty pictures?

All of the digital devices can and do communicate with each other, routinely and trivially. You can take a picture with your camera, send it from your phone, store it on your iPod. In just a few brief years, we've come to regard transactions like this as thoroughly unremarkable, but they're marvelous, really—almost miraculous. And they owe everything to the fact that all of the devices involved share the common language of on and off, yes or no, one and zero.

We too often forget this. And although I would prefer to resist determinism in any of its forms, above all the technological, it's hard to argue with in this instance. It's not simply that, as my former employers at Razorfish used to say, "Everything that can be digital, will be"; it's that everything digital can by its very nature be yoked together, and will be.

This is the logic of "convergence." Everything connects.

Thesis 27

Everyware is structurally latent in several emerging technologies.

The seemingly ineluctable logic of connection is not the only one driving the emergence of everyware. There is another type of determinism at work here, as well, harder to substantiate but no less real.

There must still be those, somewhere, who would insist that all technologies come into being neutral and uninflected, freely available for any use whatsoever. But ever since McLuhan, it's been a little difficult to take such a view seriously. A more nuanced stance would be that technologies do contain inherent potentials, gradients of connection. Each seems to fit into the puzzle that is the world in certain ways and not others.

This is not to say that social, juridical, and political forces do not exert shaping influences that are at least as significant—otherwise we really would have architected our cities around the Segway, and RU-486 would be dispensed over every drugstore counter in the land. But it wouldn't have taken a surplus of imagination, even ahead of the fact, to discern the original Napster in Paul Baran's first paper on packet-switched networks, the Manhattan skyline in the Otis safety elevator patent, or the suburb and the strip mall latent in the heart of the internal combustion engine.

Let's draw three emerging technologies from the alphabet soup of new standards and specifications we face at the moment and take a look at what they seem to "want."

First, RFID, the tiny radio-frequency transponders that are already doing so much to revolutionize logistics. The fundamental characteristic of an RFID tag is *cheapness*—as of mid-2004, the unit production cost of a standard-issue passive tag stood at about fifty cents, but industry sources are unanimous in predicting a drop below five cents in the next few years.

Somewhere around the latter price point, it becomes economic to slap tags onto just about everything: every toothbrush, every replacement windshield wiper and orange-juice carton in existence. And given how incredibly useful the things are—they readily allow the tracking, sorting, and self-identification of items they're appended to, and much more besides—there are likely to be few persuasive arguments against doing so. RFID "wants" to be everywhere and part of everything.

In networking, the next step beyond the Wi-Fi and Bluetooth standards we're familiar with is a technology called ultra-wideband (UWB), a low-power scheme that relays data at rates upwards of 500 MB/second—around ten times faster than current wireless. UWB is rich enough to support the transmission of multiple simultaneous streams of high-definition video, agile and responsive enough to facilitate ad-hoc mesh networking.* UWB wants to be the channel via which all the world's newly self-identifying artifacts transact and form spontaneous new connections.

Of course, if you want to send a message, it helps to have an address to send it to. At the moment, the prospects for anything like ubiquitous computing at the global level are starkly limited by a shortage of available addresses. But as we'll see in Section 6, the new Internet Protocol, IPv6, provides for an enormous expansion in the available address space—enough for every grain of sand on the planet to have its own IP address many times over, should such an improbable scenario ever prove desirable. Why specify such abyssal reaches of addressability, if

---

*An ad-hoc network is one that forms spontaneously, from whatever nodes are available at the moment. Mesh networking supports decentralized connectivity, with each node dynamically routing data to whichever neighbor affords the fastest connection at the moment. A scheme with both properties—self-configuring, self-healing, and highly resistant to disruption—is ideal for everyware.

not to allow every conceivable person, place, and artifact to have a comfortable spread of designators to call their own? IPv6 wants to transform everything in the world, even every part of every thing, into a node.

These are minuscule technologies, all of them: technologies of low power, low range, fine-grained resolution, and low costs. There is something in the nature of all of them that seemingly bespeaks a desire to become part of literally everything. Advertently or otherwise, we've created artifacts and standards that don't merely provide for such a thing—they almost seem to be telling us that this is what they want us to do with them.

Thesis 28

Everyware is strongly implied by the need of business for continued growth and new markets beyond the PC.

That Motorola executive recently interviewed by *The Economist* spoke the truth after all: there really *is* a need to educate consumers about "the value of a connected home and lifestyle"...to Motorola. (Not to single Motorola out, of course.)

Whether or not any one of us has asked to live in such a home, or would ever dream of pursuing such a "lifestyle," there are hard-nosed business reasons why everyware looks like a safe bet. Entire sectors of the economy are already looking to the informatic colonization of everyday things, and not merely as part of an enhanced value proposition offered the purchaser of such things. For manufacturers and vendors, the necessary gear represents quite a substantial revenue stream in its own right.

The logic of success in late capitalism is, of course, continuous growth. The trouble is that the major entertainment conglomerates and consumer-electronics manufacturers have hit something of a wall these last few years; with a few exceptions (the iPod comes to mind), we're not buying as much of their product as we used to, let alone ever more of it. Whether gaming systems, personal video recorders (PVRs), or video-enabled mobile phones, nothing has yet matched the must-have appeal of the PC, let alone reached anything like television's level of market penetration.

Putting with maximum bluntness an aspect of the ubiquitous computing scenario that is rarely attended to as closely as it ought to be: somebody has to make and sell all of the sensors and tags and chipsets and routers that together make up the everyware milieu, as well as the clothing, devices, and other artifacts incorporating them. One rather optimistic analyst sees the market for "digital home" componentry alone growing to $1 trillion worldwide by the end of the decade (yes, trillion, with a *tr*), and that doesn't include any of the other categories of ubiquitous information-processing gear we've discussed.

So if businesses from Samsung to Intel to Philips to Sony have any say in the matter, they'll do whatever they can to facilitate the advent of truly ubiquitous computing, including funding think tanks, skunk works, academic journals, and conferences devoted to it, and otherwise heavily subsidizing basic research in the field. If anything, as far as the technology and consumer-electronics industries are concerned, always-on, real-time any- and everyware can't get here fast enough.

Thesis 29

Everyware is strongly implied by the needs of an aging population in the developed world.

At the moment, those of us who live in societies of the global North are facing one of the more unusual demographic transitions ever recorded. As early childhood immunization has become near-universal over the last half-century, access to the basics of nutrition and healthcare have also become more widespread. Meanwhile, survival rates for both trauma and chronic conditions like heart disease and cancer have improved markedly, yielding to the application of medical techniques transformed, over the same stretch of time, by everything from the lessons of combat surgery, to genomics, to materials spun off from the space program, to the Internet itself.

It really is an age of everyday wonders. One reasonably foreseeable consequence of their application is a population with a notably high percentage of members over the age of sixty-five. With continued good fortune, many of them will find themselves probing the limit of human longevity, which currently seem to stand pretty much where it has for decades: somewhere around the age of 115.*

At the same time, though, with fertility rates plummeting (the populations of North America and Western Europe would already have fallen below replacement level if not for immigration, while Russia and Japan

---

*Curiously enough, after a demographic bottleneck, it is the percentage of the "oldest old" that is rising most markedly. Apparently, if you can somehow manage to survive to eighty-five, your odds of enjoying an additional ten or even twenty years are sharply improved.

shrink a little with every passing year), there are fewer and fewer young people available to take on the traditional role of looking after their elders. At least in this wide swath of the world, society as a whole is aging. For the first time, we'll get to explore the unfolding consequences of living in a gerontocracy.

This inevitably raises the question of how best to accommodate the special needs of a rapidly graying population. Unfortunately, our present arrangements—assisted-living communities, round-the-clock nursing for those who can afford it—don't scale very well, complicated by prideful reluctance or simple financial inability to accept such measures on the part of a great many. Even if everyone turning eighty wanted to and could afford to do so, neither appropriate facilities nor the qualified people to staff them exist in anything like the necessary numbers. So the remaining alternative is to try to find some way to allow people to "age in place," safely and with dignity and autonomy intact.*

A number of initiatives, from the Aware Home consortium based at the Georgia Institute of Technology to Nomura Research Institute's various "ubiquitous network" efforts, have proposed a role for ubiquitous computing in addressing the myriad challenges confronting the elderly. (If a high percentage of such proposals seem to be Japanese in origin, there's a reason: the demographic crisis is especially pressing in Japan, which is also almost certainly the society most inclined to pursue technical solutions.)

---

*Obviously, there are many alternative responses to this challenge, some of which are social or political in nature. In ubicomp circles, though, they are almost never countenanced—it rarely seems to occur to some of the parties involved that these ends might better be served by encouraging people to become caretakers through wage or benefit incentives or liberalizing immigration laws. The solution is always technical. Apparently, some of us would rather attempt to develop suitably empathetic caretaker robots than contemplate raising the minimum wage.

Some systems, though originally developed for the elderly, have broad application for use with children, the disabled, or other groups for whom simply navigating the world is a considerable challenge—for example, a wearable, RFID-based system recently described in the Japanese *Mainichi Shimbun* that automatically turns crossing signals green for elderly citizens, holding oncoming traffic until they have crossed safely.

Others are more focused on addressing the specific issues of aging. Context-aware memory augmentation—in the senses of finding missing objects, recalling long-gone circumstances to mind, and reminding someone boiling water for tea that they've left the kettle on—would help aged users manage a daily life suddenly become confusing, or even hostile. Equally importantly, such augmentation would go a long way toward helping people save face, by forestalling circumstances in which they would seem (or feel themselves to be) decrepit and forgetful.

Users with reduced vision or advanced arthritis will find voice-recognition and gesture-based interfaces far easier to use than those involving tiny buttons or narrow click targets—this will become especially critical in managing viewscreens and displays, since they may be the main source of socialization, entertainment and mental stimulation in a household. Such "universal" interfaces may be the difference that allows those with limited mobility to keep in touch with distant family members or friends in similar circumstances.

Meanwhile, the wearable biometric devices we've discussed have particular utility in geriatric telemedicine, where they can enable care centers to keep tabs on hundreds of clients at a time, monitoring them for sudden changes in critical indicators such as blood pressure and glucose level. The house itself will assume responsibility for monitoring other health-related conditions, detecting falls and similar injuries, and ensuring that users are both eating properly and taking their prescribed medication on schedule.

To so many of us, the idea of living autonomously long into old age, reasonably safe and comfortable in our own familiar surroundings, is going to be tremendously appealing, even irresistible—even if any such autonomy is underwritten by an unprecedented deployment of informatics in the home. And while nothing of the sort will happen without enormous and ongoing investment, societies may find these investments more palatable than other ways of addressing the issues they face. At least if things continue to move in the direction they're going now, societies facing the demographic transition will be hard-pressed to respond to the needs of their elders without some kind of intensive information-technological intervention.

Thesis 30

**Everyware is strongly implied by the ostensible
need for security in the post-9/11 era.**

We live, it is often said, in a surveillance society, a regime of observation
and control with tendrils that run much deeper than the camera on the
subway platform, or even the unique identifier that lets authorities trace
the movements of each transit-pass user.

If some of the specific exercises of this watchfulness originated recently—
to speak with those who came to maturity anytime before the mid-1980s
is to realize that people once showed up for flights with nothing more
than cash in hand, opened savings accounts with a single check, or were
hired without having to verify their citizenship—we know that the urge
to observe and to constrain has deep, deep roots. It waxes and wanes in
human history, sometimes hemmed in by other influences, other times
given relatively free rein.

We just happen to be living through one of the latter periods, in which the
impulse for surveillance reaches its maximum expression—its sprawling ambit in this case accommodated by the same technologies of interconnection that do so much to smooth the other aspects of our lives. If
there was any hope of this burden significantly lightening in our lifetimes,
though, it almost certainly disappeared alongside so many others, on the
morning of September 11, 2001.

The ostensible prerogatives of public safety in the post–September 11
era have been neatly summarized by curators Terence Riley and Guy
Nordenson, in their notes to the 2004 Museum of Modern Art show
"Tall Buildings," as "reduce the public sphere, restrict access, and limit
unmonitored activity." In practice, this has meant that previous ways of

doing things in the city and the world will no longer do; our fear of terror, reinscribed by the bombings in Bali, Madrid and London, has on some level forced us to reassess the commitment to mobility our open societies are based on.

This is where everyware enters the picture. At the most basic level, it would be difficult to imagine a technology more suited to monitoring a population than one sutured together from RFID, GPS, networked biometric and other sensors, and relational databases; I'd even argue that everyware redefines not merely computing but surveillance as well.*

But beyond simple observation there is control, and here too the class of information-processing systems we're discussing has a role to play. At the heart of all ambitions aimed at the curtailment of mobility is the demand that people be identifiable at all times—all else follows from that. In an everyware world, this process of identification is a much subtler and more powerful thing than we often consider it to be; when the rhythm of your footsteps or the characteristic pattern of your transactions can give you away, it's clear that we're talking about something deeper than "your papers, please."

Once this piece of information is in hand, it's possible to ask questions like Who is allowed to be here? and What is he or she allowed to do here?, questions that enable just about any defensible space to enforce its own access-control policy—not just on the level of gross admission, either, but of finely grained differential permissioning. What is currently done with guards, signage, and physical barriers ranging from velvet rope to razor wire, can still

---

*A recent Washington Post article described a current U.S. government information-gathering operation in which a citizen's "[a]ny link to the known terrorist universe—a shared address or utility account, a check deposited, [or even] a telephone call" could trigger their being investigated. The discovery of such tenuous connections is precisely what relational databases are good for, and it's why privacy experts have been sounding warnings about data mining for years. And this is before the melding of such databases with the blanket of ubiquitous awareness implied by everyware.

more effectively be accomplished when those measures are supplemented by gradients of access and permission—a "defense in depth" that has the additional appeal of being more or less subtle.

If you're having trouble getting a grip on how this would work in practice, consider the ease with which an individual's networked currency cards, transit passes and keys can be traced or disabled, remotely—in fact, this already happens.* But there's a panoply of ubiquitous security measures both actual and potential that are subtler still: navigation systems that omit all paths through an area where a National Special Security Event is transpiring, for example, or subways and buses that are automatically routed past. Elevators that won't accept requests for floors you're not accredited for; retail items, from liquor to ammunition to Sudafed, that won't let you purchase them, that simply cannot be rung up.

Context-aware differential permissioning used as a security tool will mean that certain options simply do not appear as available to you, like grayed-out items on a desktop menu—in fact, you won't get even that backhanded notification, you won't even know the options ever existed.

Such interventions are only a small sampling of the spectrum of control techniques that become available in a ubiquitously networked world. MIT sociologist Gary T. Marx sees the widest possible scope for security applications in an "engineered society" like ours, where "the goal is to eliminate or limit violations by control of the physical and social environment."

Marx identifies six broad social-engineering strategies as key to this control, and it should surprise no one that everyware facilitates them all.

- We all understand the strategy of *target removal*: "something that is not there cannot be taken," and so cash and even human-readable credit and debit cards are replaced with invisible, heavily encrypted services like PayPass.

If you purchase a New York City MetroCard with a credit or debit card, your identity is associated with it, and it can be used to track your movements. The NYPD tracked alleged rapist Peter Braunstein this way.

- *Target devaluation* seeks to make vulnerable items less desirable to those who would steal them, and this is certainly the case where self-identifying, self-describing devices or vehicles can be tracked via their network connection.
- For that matter, why even try to steal something that becomes useless in the absence of a unique biometric identifier, key or access code? This is the goal of *offender incapacitation*, a strategy also involved in attempts to lock out the purchase of denied items.
- *Target insulation* and *exclusion* are addressed via the defense in depth we've already discussed—the gauntlet of networked sensors, alarms, and cameras around any target of interest, as well as all the subtler measures that make such places harder to get to.
- And finally there is the *identification* of offenders or potential offenders, achieved via remote iris scanning or facial recognition systems like the one currently deployed in the Newham borough of London.

Who's driving the demand for ubiquitous technologies of surveillance and control? Obviously, the law-enforcement and other agencies charged with maintaining the peace, as well as various more shadowy sorts of government security apparatus. But also politicians eager to seem tough on terror, ever aware that being seen to vote in favor of enhanced security will be remembered at election time. Private security firms and rent-a-cops of all sorts. Building and facility managers with a healthy line item in their budget to provide for the acquisition of gear but neither the ongoing funds nor the authority to hire security staff. Again, the manufacturers and vendors of that gear, scenting another yawning opportunity. And never least, us, you and I, unable to forget the rubble at Ground Zero, spun senseless by routine Amber Alerts and rumors of Superdome riots, and happy for some reassurance of safety no matter how illusory.

These are obviously thorny, multisided issues, in which the legitimate prerogatives of public safety get tangled up with the sort of measures we rightfully associate with tyranny. There should be no doubt, though, that everyware's ability to facilitate the collection and leveraging of large bodies of data about a population in the context of security will be a major factor driving its appearance.

Thesis 31

Everyware is a strategy for the reduction of cognitive overload.

Happily, there are also less distressing arguments in support of everyware. One of the original motivations for conducting research into post-PC interfaces, in fact, was that they might ameliorate the sense of overload that so often attends the use of information technology.

An early culmination of this thinking was Mark Weiser and John Seely Brown's seminal "The Coming Age of Calm Technology," which argued that the ubiquity of next-generation computing would compel its designers to ensure that it "encalmed" its users. In their words, "if computers are everywhere, they better stay out of the way."

While part of Brown and Weiser's apparent stance—that designers and manufacturers would find themselves obliged to craft gentle interfaces just because it would clearly be the sensible and humane thing to do—may now strike us as naive, they were onto something.

They had elsewhere diagnosed computer-mediated information overload and its attendant stress, as some of the least salutary aspects of contemporary life. Even residing, as they then did, in an age before the widespread adoption of mobile phones in North America, they could foresee that the total cognitive burden imposed by a poorly designed ubicomp on the average, civilian user would be intolerable. (One wonders to what degree daily life at PARC in the early nineties prefigured the inbox/voicemail clamor we've all since grown so used to.) And so they set for themselves the project of how to counter such tendencies.

The strategy they devised to promote calm had to do with letting the user shift back and forth between the focus of attention and what they called the "periphery"—that which "we are attuned to without attending to explicitly." Just as, in your peripheral vision you may see objects but not need to attend to them (or even necessarily be consciously aware of their presence), here the periphery was a place where information could reside until actively required.

To design systems that "inform without overburdening," though, you'd need to call upon a different set of interface modes than the conventional PC keyboard and mouse. Brown and Weiser thought input modes like these were a big part of the problem; Roy Want and his co-authors, in a 2002 paper, flatly state that "[n]ondesktop interface modalities, such as pen, speech, vision, and touch, are attractive" to the enlightened interface designer "because they require less of a user's attention than a traditional desktop interface."*

The ideal system would be one which was imperceptible until required, in which the user's focus fell not on the tool itself but on what they were actually attempting to do with it. Were there any real-world examples of such imperceptible tools that might be offered, so that people could begin to wrap their heads around what Brown and Weiser were proposing?

One of the first things they cited happened to be a feature of the hallway right outside their offices: artist Natalie Jeremijenko's installation *Live Wire* (also known as *Dangling String*). This was an "eight-foot piece of plastic spaghetti" attached to an electric motor mounted in the ceiling that was itself wired into the building's Ethernet. Fluctuations in network traffic ran the motor, causing the string to oscillate visibly and audibly.

When traffic was low, *Live Wire* remained largely inert, but when activity surged, it would spring to life in such a way that it could both be seen

---

*The presence of "speech" on this list, and in so many depictions that come after, is interesting. Mark Weiser explicitly excluded voice-recognition interfaces from his vision of ubiquitous computing, pointing out that it would be "prominent and attention-grabbing" in precisely the way that "a good tool is not."

by hallway passers-by and heard throughout the suite of nearby offices. You might not even be consciously aware of it—you would just, somewhere in the back of your mind, register the fact that traffic was spiking. Jeremijenko's approach and the results it garnered were true to everything Brown and Weiser had speculated about the periphery.

Despite its success, this was the last anyone heard of calm technology for quite a few years; the cause wasn't taken up again until the late 1990s, when a company called Ambient Devices offered for sale something it called the Ambient Orb. The Orb was a milky globe maybe ten centimeters in diameter that communicated with a proprietary wireless network, independent of the Internet. It was supposed to sit atop a desk or a night table and use gentle modulations of color to indicate changes in some user-specified quantity, from the weather (color mapped to temperature, with the frequency of pulses indicating likelihood of precipitation) to commute traffic (green for smooth sailing, all the way through to red for "incident").

These examples are certainly more relevant to the way life is actually lived—more actionable—than a simple index of bits flowing through a network. But what if the information you're interested in is still more complex and multidimensional than that, such as the source, amount, and importance of messages piling up in your email inbox?

London-based designer/makers Jack Schulze and Matt Webb, working for Nokia, have devised a presentation called *Attention Fader* that addresses just this situation. It's a framed picture, the kind of thing you might find hanging on the side wall of an office cubicle, that appears at first glance to be a rather banal and uninflected portrait of a building along the south bank of the Thames.

But the building has a lawn before it, and a swath of sky above it, and there's a section of pathway running past, along the river embankment, and Schulze and Webb have used each of these as subtle channels for the display of useful information. Leave town for a few days, let your in-box fill up, and the number of people gaggling on the river path will slowly mount. Ignore a few high-priority messages, and first cars, then trucks, and finally tanks pull up onto the lawn; let the whole thing go, and after a while some rather malevolent-looking birds begin to circle in the sky.

But subtly, subtly. None of the crowds or trucks or birds is animated; they fade into the scene with such tact that it's difficult to say just when they arrive. It's precisely the image's apparent banality that is key to its success as a peripheral interface; it's neither loud, nor colorful, nor attention-grabbing in any obvious way. It is, rather, the kind of thing you glance up at from time to time, half-consciously, to let its message seep into your awareness. Those who see the picture at infrequent intervals mightn't notice anything but a London street scene.

Schulze and Webb's project is a paragon of encalming technology. It points clearly to a world in which the widespread deployment of information-processing resources in the environment paradoxically helps to reduce the user's sense of being overwhelmed by data. To invert Mies, here more is less.

As the global audience for computing surges past a billion, with each of those users exposed to tens or even hundreds of different technical systems in the course of a day, such encalming is going to be an appealing business case every bit as much as an ethical question for system designers. If Brown and Weiser were probably wrong as to just how strong an incentive it would provide, they were correct that the specter of global information overload would prompt at least some developers to pursue less intrusive interfaces—and these, in turn, will underwrite the further spread of everyware.

Thesis 32

Everyware is strongly implied by the continuing validity of Moore's law.

No matter what we choose to do with it, the shape that information technology takes in our lives will always be constrained by the economic and material properties of the processors undergirding it. Speed, power consumption profile, and unit production cost are going to exert enormous influence on the kinds of artifacts we build with processors and on how we use them.

Pretty much right up to the present moment, these qualities have been limiting factors on all visions involving the widespread deployment of computing devices in the environment. Processors have historically been too expensive, too delicate, and too underpowered to use in any such way, leaving computing cycles too scarce a commodity to spend on extravagances like understanding spoken commands.

As the price of processors falls dramatically, and computing power begins to permeate the world, the logic behind such parsimoniousness disappears—we can afford to spend that power freely, even lavishly, with the result that computing resources can be brought to bear on comparatively trivial tasks. We arrive at the stage where processor power can be economically devoted to addressing everyday life: As Mark Weiser put it, "where are the car keys, can I get a parking place, and is that shirt I saw last week at Macy's still on the rack?"

In fact, we know that scattering processors throughout the environment will only continue to get cheaper. The reasoning behind this assertion was first laid out in 1965 by engineer (and later Intel co-founder) Gordon Moore, in a now-legendary article in the industry journal *Electronics*. It would turn out to be one of the most profoundly influential observations in the history of computing, and as nakedly self-fulfilling a prophecy as there ever has been. (It's so well known in the industry, in fact, that if you feel like you've got a handle on what it implies for everyware, there's no reason for you not to skip ahead to Thesis 33.)

Moore's essay simply pointed out that the prevailing industry trend was for ever greater numbers of transistors to be packed into an ever smaller space, with the number of transistors per unit area approximately doubling every 24 months. He concluded almost parenthetically that the trend would continue for at least ten years into the future.

Transistor density being a fairly reliable stand-in for certain other qualities of a computer—notably, speed—this implied that future devices would offer sharply higher performance, in a smaller envelope, at a fixed cost. This "prediction" was actually a rather weak one, couched in a number of qualifiers, but nonetheless it has acquired the imposing name of "Moore's law."

Although the article never says so in so many words, Moore's law has almost universally been interpreted as a bald statement that the amount of processing power available at a given cost will double every eighteen months, indefinitely. Applied to the slightly different context of memory, the Moore curve predicts that a given amount of storage will cost roughly half as much a year and a half from now and take up half as much volume.*

That Moore's law was more or less consciously adopted as a performance goal by the chip-design industry goes a long way toward explaining the otherwise improbable fact that it still has some predictive utility after some forty years. Compare, for example, the original microprocessor,

---

*Nowhere in the annals of computing is it convincingly explained how the 24-month doubling period of Moore's original article became the 18-month period of geek legend. Moore himself insists to this day that he never used the latter number, either in his published comments or elsewhere.

Intel's 1971 4004, to a 2004 version of the same company's Pentium 4 chip: the 4004 packed 2,300 transistors and ran at a clock speed of 740 KHz, while the Pentium 4 boasts a transistor count of 178 million and runs at 3.4 GHz. That's not so far off the numbers called for by a 24-month doubling curve.

In a purely technodeterminist reading, anyway, Moore's law tells us exactly where we're headed next. It's true that Gordon Moore made his observation in the long-ago of 1965, and so one might be forgiven for thinking that his "law" had little left to tell us. But as far as anyone knowledgeable can tell, its limits are a long way off. A vocal minority continues to assert the belief that even after the photolithography used in chip fabrication hits the limits inherent in matter, more exotic methods will allow the extension of Moore's unprecedented run. Whether or not Moore's law can be extended indefinitely, there is sufficient reason to believe that information-processing componentry will keep getting smaller, cheaper, and more powerful for some time yet to come.

Because processors will be so ridiculously cheap, the world can be seeded with them economically. Because their cheapness will mean their disposability, they'll be installed in places it wouldn't have made sense to put them before—light switches, sneakers, milk cartons. There will be so very, very many of them—thousands of them devoted to every person and place—that it won't really matter whether some percentage of them fail. They will be both powerful individually, and able to share computation among themselves besides, and able to parse the complexities presented by problems of everyday life. Whatever name it is called by, however little it may resemble the calm technology envisioned by Mark Weiser, a computing with these properties will effectively be ubiquitous, in any meaningful sense of the word.

Thesis 33

The appeal of everyware is at some level universal.

Be honest now: Who among us has not wished, from time to time, for some powerful sympathetic agency to intervene in our lives, to fix our mistakes and rescue us from the consequences of our lapses in judgment?

This is one desire I sense, beneath all the various projects devoted to ubiquitous surveillance or memory augmentation or encalming. What are they if not dreams of welcome and safety, of some cushion against the buffeting of our times? What are they if not a promise of some awareness in the world other than our own, infused into everything around us, capable of autonomous action and dedicated to our well-being?

In a sense this is only a return to a much older tradition. For most of our sojourn on this planet, human beings have understood the physical world as a place intensely invested with consciousness and agency; the idea that the world is alive, that the objects therein are sentient and can be transacted with, is old and deep and so common to all the cultures of humanity that it may as well be called universal.

As Freud described it, "the world was full of spirits...and all the objects in the external world were their dwelling-place, or perhaps identical with them." It is only comparatively recently that most people have believed otherwise—indeed, most of the humans who ever walked the planet would have found it utter folly to conceive of the natural world as mainstream Western culture did until very recently: a passive, inert, purely material stage, on which the only meaningful actors are human ones.

If we have always acted as though the things around us are alive, then the will to make it so in fact (or at least make it seem so) at the moment the technical wherewithal became available is understandable. That things like gestural and voice-recognition interfaces are so fervently pursued despite the many difficulties involved in perfecting them might tell us something about the deep roots of their appeal, if we're willing to listen.

Their long pedigree in science fiction merely extends the earlier tradition; folklore is replete with caves that open at a spoken command, swords that can be claimed only by a single individual, mirrors that answer with killing honesty when asked to name the fairest maiden in the land, and so on. Why, then, should anyone be surprised when we try to restage these tales, this time with our technology in the central role? Everyware is simply speaking to something that has lain dormant within us for much of modernity and played an overt, daily role in our lives for a very long time before that.

This is perhaps the most poignant factor driving the development of everyware, but as we've seen, it is far from the only one. From the crassest of motives to the noblest, there are so many powerful forces converging on the same set of technical solutions that their eventual realization truly does seem inevitable, no matter how we may quail at the determinism implied.

We will get to make meaningful choices about the precise shape of their appearance in the world, however—but only if we are smarter and more prudent than we have been about previous technologies. The next section will cover some of the issues we will need to keep foremost in mind if we want to make these crucial decisions wisely.

What are the issues we need to be aware of?

If we have by now concluded that some kind of everyware does seem inevitable, the precise form that it will take in our lives is still contingent, open to change.

What are some of the issues we need to be aware of, in order to make the sort of wise decisions that will shape its emergence in congenial ways?

Thesis 34

Everyware insinuates itself into transactions never before subject to technical intervention.

Even if you yourself are not a connoisseur of gourmet bathing experiences, you may be interested to learn that the Brazilian company IHOUSE last year offered for sale something it called the Smart Hydro "intelligent bathtub."

The Smart Hydro is a preview of the experience that awaits us in the fully networked home, at least at the high end of the market. It really puts the bather in the driver's seat, as it were, giving its user access to a range of preference settings, from the essentials of water temperature and level to treats like "bath essence or foam, a variety of hydromassage programs and even light intensity." It can even be programmed to fill itself and then call you on your mobile phone mid-commute, just to let you know that your bath will be ready for you the moment you step through the door. (Of course it will be "[kept] temperature controlled until you arrive home.")

But you already knew how to draw a bath, didn't you? And you've somehow survived this far in life without the help of automated calls from the bathroom infrastructure. In fact, learning how to manage your bathtub's preference settings is probably not on the list of things you most want to do with your time—not when you've pretty much had a handle on the situation since the age of five or six.

Especially as a consequence of its insinuation into everyday life, everyware appears in all kinds of transactions that have never before been subject to highly technical intervention. Ubicomp advocate Mike Kuniavsky acknowledges this in his "Smart Furniture Manifesto": in his own words, endowing furniture and other everyday things with digital intelligence "can introduce all kinds of complexity and failure modes that don't currently exist." (I'd argue that you can replace the "can" in that sentence with "demonstrably will.")

The consequences of such complexification extend beyond bathing, or the similarly simple but profound pleasures of hearth and table, to implicate a further set of experiences that tend to be the most meaningful and special to us.

Take friendship. Current social-networking applications, like Orkut or Friendster, already offer us digital profiles of the people we know. An ambient version—and such systems have been proposed—could interpose these profiles in real time, augmenting the first glimpse of an acquaintance with an overlay of their name, a list of the friends we have in common, and an indication of how warmly we regard them. The benefit *qua* memory augmentation is obvious, perfect for those of us who always feel more than a little guilty about forgetting someone's name. But doesn't this begin to redefine what it means to "recognize" or to "know" someone? (We'll see in the next thesis that such a degree of explicitness poses significant challenges socially as well as semantically.)

Take exercise, or play, or sexuality, all of which will surely become sites of intense mediation in a fully developed everyware milieu. Something as simple as hiking in the wilderness becomes almost unrecognizable when overlaid with GPS location, sophisticated visual pattern-recognition algorithms, and the content of networked geological, botanical, and zoological databases—you won't get lost, surely, or mistake poisonous mushrooms for the edible varieties, but it could hardly be said that you're "getting away from it all."

Even meditation is transformed into something new and different: since we know empirically that the brains of Tibetan monks in deep contemplation show regular alpha-wave patterns, it's easy to imagine environmental interventions, from light to sound to airflow to scent, designed to evoke the state of mindfulness, coupled to a body-monitor setting that helps you recognize when you've entered it.

If these scenarios present us with reason to be concerned about ubiquitous interventions, this doesn't necessarily mean we should forgo all such attempts to invest the world with computational power. It simply means that we have to be unusually careful about what we're doing, more careful certainly than we've been in the past. Because by and large, whatever frustrations our sojourns in the world present us with, we've had a long time to get used to them; to paraphrase Paul Robeson, we suits ourselves. Whatever marginal "improvement" is enacted by overlaying daily life with digital mediation has to be balanced against the risk of screwing up something that already works, however gracelessly or inelegantly.

Eliel Saarinen—Eero's father, and a professor of architecture in his own right—invariably reminded his students that they must "[a]lways design a thing by considering it in its next larger context." The implications of this line of thought for everyware are obvious: In some particularly delicate circumstances, it would probably be wisest to leave well enough alone.

Thesis 35

Everyware surfaces and makes explicit information that has always been latent in our lives, and this will frequently be incommensurate with social or psychological comfort.

Remember BodyMedia, the company responsible for the conformal, Band-Aid–sized SenseWear sensor? BodyMedia's vice president for product design, Chris Kasabach, says the company thinks of the living body as a "continuous beacon": "signals can either fall on the floor, or you can collect them and they can tell you something higher-level" about the organism in question.

Stripped of its specific referent, this is as good a one-sentence description of the data-discovery aspect of everyware as you are ever likely to come across. Everyware's mesh of enhanced objects dispersed throughout everyday life also happens to offer a way of collecting the signals already out there and making of them a gnosis of the world.

In the case of the body especially, these signals have always been there. All that's really new about SenseWear is the conjoined ambition and practical wherewithal to capture and interpret such signals—and to make use of them. This is true of many things. The world is increasingly becoming a place where any given fact is subject to both quantification and publication—and not merely those captured by the various kinds of sensors we encounter, but also ones that you or I have volunteered.

The truth of this was driven home by the first online social-networking sites. Those of us who used early versions of Friendster, Orkut, or LinkedIn will understand what I mean when I say they occasionally made uncomfortably explicit certain aspects of our social relationships that we generally prefer to keep shrouded in ambiguity: I like her better than him; she thinks I'm highly reliable and even very cool, but not at all sexy; I want to be seen and understood as an associate of yours, but not of his.

Even services with other primary objectives observe such social differentiation these days. The Flickr photo-sharing service, for example, recognizes a gradient of affinity, inscribing distinctions between a user's "family," "friends," "contacts," and everyone else—with the result that there's plenty of room for people who know me on Flickr to wonder why (and potentially be hurt by the fact that) I consider them a "contact" and not a "friend."

What if *every* fact about which we generally try to dissemble, in our crafting of a mask to show the world, was instead made readily and transparently available? I'm not just talking about obvious privacy issues—histories of various sorts of irresponsibility, or of unpopular political, religious, or sexual predilections—but about subtler and seemingly harmless things as well: who you've chosen to befriend in your life, say, or what kinds of intimacy you choose to share with them, but not others.

This is exactly what is implied by a global information processing system with inputs and outputs scattered all over the place. With everyware, all that information about you or me going into the network implies that it comes out again somewhere else—a "somewhere" that is difficult or impossible to specify ahead of time—and this has real consequences for how we go about constructing a social self. When these private and unspoken arrangements are drawn out into the open, are made public and explicit, embarrassment, discomfort, even resentment can follow for all parties involved.

These are events that Gary T. Marx, the MIT professor emeritus of sociology whose theories of technology and social control we discussed in Thesis 30, refers to as *border crossings*: irruptions of information in an unexpected (and generally problematic) context. Marx identifies several distinct types of crossing—natural, social, spatial/temporal, and ephemeral—but they all share a common nature: in each case, something happens to violate "the expectation by people that parts of their lives can exist in isolation from other parts." You see something compromising through a hole in your neighbor's fence, for example, or a mother sneaks into her daughter's room and reads her "secret" diary.

The Web is a generator par excellence of such crossings, from the ludicrous to the terrifying. We've all seen a momentary slip of the tongue recorded on high-fidelity video and uploaded for all the world to see (and mock). There's an entire genre of humor revolving around the sundry Jedi Knight fantasies and wardrobe malfunctions that shall now live for all time, mirrored on dozens or hundreds of servers around the globe. And much of the annoyance of spam, for many of us, is the appearance of sexually explicit language and/or imagery in times and places we've devoted to other activities.

But this is all a foretaste of what we can see coming. Where everyware is concerned, we can no longer expect *anything* to exist in isolation from anything else. It comprises a "global mnemotechnical system," in the words of French philosopher Bernard Stiegler—a mesh of computational awareness, operating in a great many places and on a great many channels, fused to techniques that permit the relational or semantic cross-referencing of the facts thus garnered, and an almost limitless variety of modes and opportunities for output. It brings along with it the certainty that if a fact once enters the grid—any fact, of any sort, from your Aunt Helga's blood pressure at noon last Sunday to the way you currently feel about your most recent ex-boyfriend—it will acquire a strange kind of immortality.

Unable, apparently, to bear the idea that our signals might "fall on the floor," we've arranged to capture them for all time, uploading them to a net where they will bounce from one node, to another, to another—for as long as there remains a network to hold them.

One trouble with this is that we've historically built our notions of reputation such that they rely on *exformation*—on certain kinds of information leaving the world, disappearing from accessibility. But with such mnemotechnical systems in place, information never *does* leave the world. It just keeps accumulating, simultaneously more explicit, more available, and more persistent than anything we or our societies have yet reckoned with.

Thesis 36

Latent information is also made explicit as a result of the conventions suggested by everyware.

Latent data pops to the surface in everyware as a result of new conventions, every bit as much as of new systems. These are ways of thinking about the world that follow in the wake of the mass adoption of information technology, as natural afterward as they would have seemed alien beforehand.

For example, designers Ulla-Maaria Mutanen and Jyri Engeström, working with economics student Adam Wern, have proposed something they call a "free product identifier." Their ThingLinks offer an equivalent of the familiar UPC or ISBN codes, specifically designed for the "invisible tail" of short-run, amateur, or folk productions previously denied a place in the grand electronic souk of late capitalism. Anyone, at no charge, can generate a code, associate it with an object, and fill out some basic information relating to it, and forever after that object can be looked up via the net—either the one we enjoy now, or whatever ubiquitous variant comes afterward.*

On the one hand, this is a truly utopian gesture. As a manifestation of the emerging culture of mass amateurization, such open codes would allow small-scale producers—from West Berkeley sculptors to Bangladeshi weaving collectives—to compete on something approaching the same ground as professional manufacturers and distributors.

Each ThingLink is technically a valid Uniform Resource Identifier, albeit one refined down to the "scheme" and "path" semantic elements.

At the same time, though, and despite its designers' clear intentions, a free product identifier could be regarded as a harbinger of the insidious transformation of just about everything into machine-readable information.

Such an identifier is not a technical system in the usual sense. It is intangible, nonmaterial. It's nothing more than a convention: a format and perhaps some protocols for handling information expressed in that format. But its shape and conception are strongly conditioned by the existence of parallel conventions—conventions that *are* embodied in specific technologies. The whole notion of a Uniform Resource Identifier, for example, which was called into being by the Internet, or a Universal Product Code, which cannot be separated from the technics of bar-coding and its descendent, RFID.

And though such conventions may be intangible, they nevertheless have power, in our minds and in the world. The existence of a machine-readable format for object identification, particularly, is a container waiting to be filled, and our awareness that such a thing exists will transform the way we understand the situations around us. Because once we've internalized the notion, any object that might once have had an independent existence—unobserved by anyone outside its immediate physical vicinity, unrecorded and certainly uncorrelated—can be captured and recast as a node.

Once again, we see latent facts about the world brought to the surface and made available to our networked mnemotechnical systems—this time, through the existence of a convention, rather than a type or particular deployment of technology. Ubiquitous, then, does turn out to mean exactly that.

Thesis 37

Everyday life presents designers of everyware with a particularly difficult case because so very much about it is tacit, unspoken, or defined with insufficient precision.

One of the reasons why networked bathtubs, explicitly ordered friendship arrays, and the other artifacts of everyware we've encountered can seem so dissonant to us is that they collapse two realms that have generally been separate and distinct in the past: the technical, with all the ordered precision it implies, and the messy inexactitude of the everyday.

Everyday situations pose a particular challenge to the designer because so many of their important constituents are tacit or unspoken. They lack hard edges, clear definitions, known sets of actors, and defined time limits, and this makes them exquisitely difficult to represent in terms useful to system engineers. Significant aspects of a given transaction may not even be consciously perceived by participants, in the way that things seen too often disappear from sight.

Information technology, of course, requires just the opposite: that as much as possible be made as explicit as possible. In programming, for example, software engineers use tools like Object Management Group's Unified Modeling Language (UML) to specify application structure, behavior and architecture with the necessary degree of rigor. (UML and its analogues can also be used to map less technical procedures, e.g., business processes.)

Make no mistake about it, "specify" is the operative word here. UML allows programmers to decompose a situation into a use case: a highly granular, stepped, sequential representation of the interaction, with all events and participants precisely defined. Such use cases are a necessary intermediate step between the high-level, natural language description of a scenario and its ultimate expression in code.

In a valid use case, nothing is left unspecified or undefined. Every party to an interaction must be named, as well as all of the attributes belonging to (and all the operations that can be performed on) each of them. To an non-engineer, the level of attention to detail involved can seem almost pathologically obsessive. In order to write sound code, though, all of these values must be specified minutely.

Now consider such requirements in the light of everyday life—specifically, in the light of those everyday communications that appear to lack content, but which nonetheless convey important social and emotional information: so-called *phatic* utterances. These present us with a perfect example of something critical to our understanding of everyday life, which is yet highly resistant to technical specification.

We're familiar with quite a few kinds of phatic utterance, from morning greetings in the elevator, or the flurry of endearments with which happy couples shower each other, to "minimal verbal encouragers"—the odd grunts and "uh-huh"s that let you know when someone is listening to you. Responding appropriately to such communications means accurately picking up subtle cues as to the communicator's intent, and those cues are often nonverbal in nature. They may reside in the speaker's body language, or in the context in which the utterance is offered. Either way, though, we understand that when a neighbor says "Lovely weather we're having, isn't it?," this is a performance of openness, availability, and friendliness, not an invitation to discuss the climate.

Most nonautistic adults have internalized the complexities of parsing situations like these, but designers of technical systems will find them very, very difficult to represent adequately. And if phatic speech poses real problems, at least it *is* speech. What about the pauses, ellipses, pregnant silences, and other signifying absences of everyday communication? How do you model profoundly meaningful but essentially negative events like these in UML?

This isn't a rhetorical question. The fuzziness, indirection and imprecision we see in everyday speech are far from atypical; they can stand in for many human behaviors that are not exactly what they seem, many situations whose meaning is the product of an extremely subtle interplay among events both tacit and fully articulated.

If we are ever to regard the appearance of computing in everyday life as anything more than an annoyance, though, someone will have to do just this sort of thing. Someone will have to model fuzzy, indirect, imprecise behaviors. Someone will have to teach systems to regard some utterances as signal and some as noise, some facts as significant and some as misdirection, some gestures as compulsive tics and yet others as meaningful commands.

These are clearly not trivial things to expect. In fact, challenges of this order are often called "AI-hard"—that is, a system capable of mastering them could be construed as having successfully met the definition of artificial human intelligence. Simply describing everyday situations in useful detail would utterly tax contemporary digital design practice and most of the methodological tools it's built on.

Again, I am not expressing the sentiment that we should not attempt to design systems graceful enough for everyday life. I am simply trying to evoke the magnitude of the challenges faced by the designers of such systems. If nothing else, it would be wise for us all to remember that, while our information technology may be digital in nature, the human beings interacting with it will always be infuriatingly and delightfully analog.

Thesis 38

Everyware is problematic because it is hard to see literally.

Like bio- and nanotechnology, everyware is a contemporary technics whose physical traces can be difficult or even impossible to see with the unaided eye.

It's a minuscule technology. Its material constituents are for the most part sensors, processors, and memory chips of centimeter scale or smaller, connected (where they require physical connections at all) via printed, woven, or otherwise conformal circuitry.

It's a dissembling technology: those constituents are embedded in objects whose outer form may offer no clue as to their functionality.

It's also, of course, a wireless technology, its calls and responses riding through the environment on modulated radio waves.

All of these qualities make everyware quite hard to discern in its particulars—especially as compared to earlier computing paradigms with their obvious outcroppings of High Technology.

We should get used to the idea that there will henceforth be little correlation between the appearance of an artifact and its capabilities—no obvious indications as to how to invoke basic functionality nor that the artifact is capable of doing anything at all. When even a space that appears entirely empty may in fact contain—to all intents, may *be*—a powerful information processing system, we can no longer rely on appearances to guide us.

Thesis 39

Everyware is problematic because it is hard to see figuratively.

If its physical constituents are literally too small, too deeply buried, or too intangible to be made out with the eye, there are also other (and potentially still more decisive) ways in which everyware is hard to see clearly.

This quality of imperceptibility is not simply a general property of ubiquitous systems; for the most part, rather, it's something that has deliberately been sought and worked toward. As we've seen, the sleight of hand by which information processing appears to dissolve into everyday behavior is by no means easy to achieve.

There are two sides of this, of course. On the one hand, this is what Mark Weiser and John Seely Brown set out as the goal of their "calm technology": interfaces that do not call undue attention to themselves, interactions that are allowed to remain peripheral. If a Weiserian calm technology appears as the result of a consciously pursued strategy of disappearance, it does so because its designers believed that this was the best way to relieve the stress engendered by more overt and attention-compelling interfaces.

But if they contain enormous potential for good, such disappearances can also conceal what precisely is at issue in a given transaction, who stands to benefit from it and whose interests are at risk. MasterCard, for example, clearly hopes that people will lose track of what is signified by the tap of a PayPass card—that the action will become automatic and thus fade from perception. In one field test, users of PayPass-enabled devices—in this case, key fobs and cell phones—spent 25 percent more than those using cash. ("Just tap & go," indeed.)

As computing technology becomes less overt and less conspicuous, it gets harder to see that devices are designed, manufactured, and marketed by some specific institution, that network and interface standards are specified by some body, and so on. A laptop is clearly made by Toshiba or Dell or Apple, but what about a situation?

This is the flipside of the seeming inevitability we've considered, the argument against technodeterminism. Despite the attributes that appear to inhere in technologies even at the very moment that they come into being, there is always human agency involved—always. So if RFID "wants" to be everywhere and part of everything, if IPv6 "wants" to transform everything in the world into a node, we should remember to ask: Who designed them to be that way? Who specified a networking protocol or an address space with these features, and why did they make these decisions and not others?

Historically, its opacity to the nonspecialist has lent technological development an entirely undeserved aura of inevitability, which in turn has tended to obscure questions of agency and accountability. This is only exacerbated in the case of a technology that is also literally bordering on the imperceptible.

Most difficult of all is the case when we cease to think of some tool as being "technology" at all—as studies in Japan and Norway indicate is currently true of mobile phones, at least in those places. Under such circumstances, the technology's governing metaphors and assumptions have an easier time infiltrating the other decisions we make about the world. Their effects come to seem more normal, more natural, simply the way things are done, while gestures of refusal become that much harder to make or to justify. And that is something that should give us pause, at the cusp of our embrace of something as insinuative and as hard to see as everyware.

Thesis 40

The discourse of seamlessness effaces or elides meaningful distinctions between systems.

Closely related to the question of everyware's imperceptibility is its *seamlessness*. This is the idea that both the inner workings of a given system and its junctures with others should be imperceptible to the user, and it's been extraordinarily influential in ubicomp circles over the last eight or ten years. In fact, seamless has become one of those words that one rarely hears except in the context of phrases like "seamless interaction," "seamless integration," "seamless interconnection," or "seamless interfaces."

The notion inarguably has a pedigree in the field; the term itself goes straight back to the ubiquitous Mark Weiser. Ironically enough, though, given its later widespread currency, Weiser regarded seamlessness as an undesirable and fundamentally homogenizing attribute in a ubiquitous system.

Without seams, after all, it's hard to tell where one thing ends and something else begins—points of difference and distinction tend to be smoothed over or flattened out. Very much alive to this danger, Weiser advocated the alternative concept of "seamfulness, with beautiful seams," in which users are helped to understand the systems they encounter, how they work, and what happens at their junctures with one another by the design of the systems themselves.

However rewarding, properly providing the user with seamful experiences is obviously a rather time-consuming and difficult way to go about doing things. Maybe this is why Matthew Chalmers and Ian MacColl, then of the University of Glasgow, found in 2003 that Weiser's musings had been oddly inverted in the process of their reification. Phrases invoking seamlessness positively peppered the ubicomp literature they surveyed, from

IBM's pervasive computing Web site to the EU's prospectus for its Disappearing Computer initiative—and where the idea appeared in such material, it was generally presented as an unquestioned good and a goal to which the whole ubicomp community should aspire.

Chalmers and MacColl decided to reintroduce the notion of beautiful seams, challenging the whole discourse of smooth continuity they found to be endemic in contemporary models of ubicomp. But while they were among the earliest critics of seamlessness, they were far from alone in their discomfort with the notion, at least if the frequency with which their work on seamful design is cited is any indication.

Critics were motivated by several apparent flaws in the staging of seamless presentations. The most obvious was dishonesty: The infrastructure supporting the user's experience is deeply heterogeneous, and, at least in contemporary, real-world systems, frequently enough held together by the digital equivalent of duct tape and chewing gum. In Chalmers and MacColl's words, ubiquitous devices and infrastructural components "have limited sampling rates and resolution, are prone to communication delays and disconnections, have finite data storage limits and have representational schemes of finite scope and accuracy"; any attempt to provide the user with a continuous experience must somehow paper over these circumstances.

More worrisome than simple dishonesty, though, is the paternalism involved: seamlessness deprives the user of meaningful participation in the decisions that affect his or her experience. The example often given by Chalmers, in his discussion of the distinctions between seamlessness and its inverse, is that of a mobile phone user: In most such cases, information such as differentials in signal strength between adjacent cells, or the location of boundaries at which a phone is "handed over" from one cell to another, is inaccessible, handled automatically at a level beneath presentation in the interface.

While such information is probably useless, or even annoying, to most users at most times, it surely might prove desirable for some users at some times. By extension, most ubiquitous systems will involve the sort of complexity that designers are ordinarily tempted to sweep under the rug, secure in the wisdom that "users don't care about that." No matter how correct this determination may be in most cases, or how well-intentioned the effort to shield the user, there should always be some accommodation for those wishing to bring the full scope of a system's complexity to light.

Another critical flaw in seamlessness was also first raised by Chalmers and MacColl, and it related to the question of *appropriation*. Drawing on the earlier work of Paul Dourish and Steve Harrison, they questioned whether a system that was presented to users as seamless could ever afford those users the sense of ownership so critical to rewarding experiences of technology.

Dourish and Harrison offered as an object lesson the distinction between two early videoconferencing systems, from Bellcore Labs and Xerox PARC. The Bellcore system, VideoWindow, was an extremely sophisticated effort in supporting "copresence"; it was complex and expensive, and it presented itself to users monolithically. In Dourish and Harrison's words, "it wasn't theirs, and they could not make it theirs." By contrast, users could and did play with the Xerox system, based as it was on cheap, portable cameras. Predictably enough, those who used the Xerox effort found that it "offered something wonderful," while the designers of VideoWindow could only lamely conclude from their disappointing trials that their system "lack[ed] something due to factors we do not understand."

Chalmers and MacColl drew from this the inference that systems presented as seamless would be difficult to appropriate, claim and customize in the ways that seem to make people happiest. Visible seams, by contrast, expose the places where users can "reach into" a system and tune it to their preference.

The resonance of such critiques will only grow as ubiquitous systems get closer to everyday reality, because the discourse of seamlessness continues to hold sway in the field. Consider how they might play out in the relationship between two notional data-collection systems, biometric in nature, one of which operates at the household level and the other at some ambiguously larger scale.

You own the local system, whose tendrils reach from your refrigerator to the bathroom scale to the exercise monitor you wear to the gym. While it is constantly deriving precise numeric values for attributes like caloric intake and body-mass index, its findings are delivered to you not as raw data, but as gentle, high-level comments that appear on the bathroom mirror and the refrigerator door: "Run an extra ten minutes this morning," or "Try adding leafy greens to today's meals."

And while most of us, for obvious reasons, would not want something like this directly connected with the outside world, in this case your health-management system is interfaced with your household-management system. And it is the *latter* that is coupled, at levels beneath your awareness, to larger, external information-gathering efforts—those belonging to insurance companies, or marketers, or the Department of Health and Human Services.

These are two different manifestations of seamlessness, and both interfere with your ability to regulate the flow of information around you. Maybe you're actually curious to know exactly how many calories you burned today. More seriously, of course, is the problem posed by the obscure interconnection of apparently discrete systems. There we run into the same issue we saw with PayPass: that the decision made to shield the user from the system's workings also conceals who is at risk and who stands to benefit in a given transaction.

Given these potentials, there's something refreshing about the notion of making the seams and junctions that hold our technologies together at least optionally visible. In some sense, doing so would demolish the magical sense of effortlessness so many theories of ubiquitous design aim for, but that could always be switched back on, couldn't it?

I like the honesty of seamfulness, the way it invites users to participate in a narrative from which they had been foreclosed. In everyware as in life, good fences make good neighbors.

Thesis 41

Before they are knit together, the systems that comprise everyware may appear to be relatively conventional, with well-understood interfaces and affordances. When interconnected, they will assuredly interact in emergent and unpredictable ways.

Our information technology is difficult to consider holistically, because it is modular: Though its constituents work together, they are designed at different times, in different places, by different parties, to different ends. Furthermore, these constituents are agnostic as to the circumstances of their use: A database doesn't "care" whether it's used to enhance a rental car company's relationships with its best customers, manage a public housing authority's inventory of cleaning supplies, or keep tabs on the members of a particular ethnic group scattered through a larger population.

This modularity has historically been the very strength of information technology, at least in the years since the Internet raised notions of standardization and interoperability to wide currency in the industry. It lends our informatic systems an enormous degree of flexibility, adaptability, even vigor, and it will and should continue to do so.

But in our experiences of everyware, we'll also find that modularity will occasionally prove to be the cause of concern. Even where we recognize that certain high-level effects of ubiquitous systems are less comfortable for users than we might like, it will generally not be possible to address these effects at the level of component artifacts. Apart from those of literal imperceptibility, almost all of the issues we're interested in—the surfacing of previously latent information, the persistence lent ephemera by their encoding in mnemotechnical systems, certainly seamlessness—do not arise as a result of properties residing in components themselves. They are, rather, an emergent property of the components' interaction, of their deployment in the world in specific patterns and combinations.

This is a thoroughly conventional microcontroller. This is an off-the-shelf microphone. This is a stock door-actuator mechanism. We think we know them thoroughly, understand their properties and characteristics in detail, and under most circumstances, that is a reasonably safe assumption. But put them together properly, embed them in the world in a particular relationship with each other, and we have a system that closes a door between two spaces any time the sound level in one of them breaches a certain threshold. And though the exact details will vary depending on where and how it is deployed, this system will have behaviors and consequences that absolutely could not have been predicted by someone considering the components beforehand—no matter how expert or insightful that person might be.

Maybe this strikes you as trivial. Consider, then, a somewhat more baroque but no less credible scenario: Contributions to political campaigns, at least in the United States, are already a matter of public record, stored in databases that are easily accessible on the Internet.* And we've known from as far back as Smart Floor that unconscious aspects of a person's gait—things like weight distribution and tread period—can not only be sensed, but can also serve as a surprisingly accurate identifier, at least when a great many data points are gathered. (As the Georgia Tech team responsible for Smart Floor rather disingenuously asked, "Why not make the floor 'smart,' and use it to identify and track people?")

On the surface, these seem like two thoroughly unrelated factoids about the world we live in, so much so that the third sentence of the paragraph

---

*The source I happen to be thinking of is opensecrets.org, but there are many others. See spywareguide.com for some interesting mash-ups and combinations.

above almost reads like a non sequitur. But connect the two discrete databases, design software that draws inferences from the appearance of certain patterns of fact—as our relational technology certainly allows us to do—and we have a situation where you can be identified *by name and likely political sympathy* as you walk through a space provisioned with the necessary sensors.

Did anyone intend this? Of course not—at least, we can assume that the original designers of each separate system did not. But when things like sensors and databases are networked and interoperable, agnostic and freely available, it is a straightforward matter to combine them to produce effects unforeseen by their creators.

The Smart Floor example is, of course, deliberately provocative; there's nothing in the literature to suggest that Georgia Tech's gait-recognition system was ever scaled up to work in high-traffic public spaces, let alone that any spaces beyond their own lab were ever instrumented in this way. Nevertheless, there is nothing in the scenario that could not in principle be done tomorrow.

We should never make the mistake of believing, as designers, users or policymakers, that we understand exactly what we're dealing with in an abstract discussion of everyware. How can we fully understand, let alone propose to regulate, a technology whose important consequences may only arise combinatorially as a result of its specific placement in the world?

I believe that in the fullness of time, the emergent behavior of ubiquitous systems will present us and our societies with the deepest of challenges. Such behavior will raise the specter of autonomous artifacts, even call into question the proper degree of loyalty an object should have toward its owners or users. As real as these issues are, though, we're not quite there yet; perhaps it would be wiser to deal with the foreseeable implications of near-term systems before addressing the problems that await us a few steps further out.

Thesis 42

In everyware, many issues are decided at the level of architecture, and therefore do not admit to any substantive recourse in real time.

Stanford law professor Lawrence Lessig argues, in his book *Code and Other Laws of Cyberspace*, that the deep structural design of informatic systems—their architecture—has important implications for the degree of freedom people are allowed in using those systems, forever after. Whether consciously or not, values are encoded into a technology, in preference to others that might have been, and then enacted whenever the technology is employed.

For example, the Internet was originally designed so that the network itself knows nothing about the systems connected to it, other than the fact that each has a valid address and handles the appropriate protocols. It could have been designed differently, but it wasn't. Somebody made the decision that the cause of optimal network efficiency was best served by such an "end-to-end" architecture.*

Lessig believes that this engineering decision has had the profoundest consequences for the way we present ourselves on the net and for the regulability of our behavior there. Among other things, "in real space... anonymity has to be created, but in cyberspace anonymity is the given." And so some rather high-level behaviors—from leaving unsigned comments on a Web site, to being able to download a movie to a local

---

In this case, the identity of the "somebody" in question is widely known: The relevant design decisions were set forth by Robert E. Kahn and Vint Cerf, in a 1974 paper called A Protocol for Packet Network Intercommunication. *The identity of responsible parties will not always be so transparent.*

machine, traceable to nothing more substantial than an IP address—are underwritten by a decision made years before, concerning the interaction of host machines at the network layer.

We needn't go quite that deep to get to a level where the design of a particular technical system winds up inscribing some set of values in the world.

Imagine that a large American company—say, an automobile manufacturer—adopts a requirement that its employees carry RFID-tagged personal identification. After a lengthy acquisition process, the company selects a vendor to provide the ID cards and their associated paraphernalia—card encoders and readers, management software, and the like.

As it happens, this particular identification system has been designed to be as flexible and generic as possible, so as to appeal to the largest pool of potential adopters. Its designers have therefore provided it with the ability to encode a wide range of attributes about a card holder—ethnicity, sex, age, and dozens of others. Although the automotive company itself never uses these fields, every card carried nevertheless has the technical ability to record such facts about its bearer.

And then suppose that—largely as a consequence of the automobile manufacturer's successful and public large-scale roll-out of the system—this identification system is adopted by a wide variety of other institutions, private and public. In fact, with minor modifications, it's embraced as the standard driver's license schema by a number of states. And because the various state DMVs collect such data, and the ID-generation system affords them the technical ability to do so, the new licenses wind up inscribed with machine-readable data about the bearer's sex, height, weight and other physical characteristics, ethnicity....

If you're having a hard time swallowing this set-up, consider that history is chock-full of situations where some convention originally developed for one application was adopted as a de facto standard elsewhere. For our purposes, the prime example is the Social Security number, which was never supposed to be a national identity number—in fact, it was precisely this fear that nearly torpedoed its adoption, in 1936.

By 1961, however, when the Internal Revenue Service adopted the Social Security number as a unique identifier, such fears had apparently faded. At present, institutions both public (the armed forces) and private (banks, hospitals, universities) routinely use the SSN in place of their own numeric identification standards. So there's ample justification not to be terribly impressed by protestations that things like this "could never happen."

We see that a structural decision made for business purposes—i.e., the ability given each card to record a lengthy list of attributes about the person carrying it—eventually winds up providing the state with an identity card schema that reflects those attributes, which it can then compel citizens to carry. What's more, private parties equipped with a standard, off-the-shelf reader now have the ability to detect such attributes, and program other, interlinked systems to respond to them.

Closing the loop, what happens when a building's owners decide that they'd rather not have people of a given age group or ethnicity on the premises? What happens if such a lock-out setting is enabled, even temporarily and accidentally?*

No single choice in this chain, until the very last, was made with anything but the proverbial good intentions. The logic of each seemed reasonable, even unassailable, at the time it was made. But the clear result is that now the world has been provisioned with a system capable of the worst sort of discriminatory exclusion, and doing it all cold-bloodedly, at the level of its architecture.

Such decisions are essentially uncontestable. In this situation, the person denied access has no effective recourse in real time—such options that do exist take time and effort to enact. Even if we are eventually able to challenge the terms of the situation—whether by appealing to a human attendant who happens to be standing by, hacking into the

---

*It's worth noting, in this context, that the fundamentalist-Christian putsch in Margaret Atwood's 1986 The Handmaid's Tale is at least in part accomplished by first installing a ubiquitous, nationwide banking network and then locking out all users whose profiles identify them as female.

system ourselves, complaining to the ACLU, or mounting a class-action lawsuit—the burden of time and energy invested in such activism falls squarely on our own shoulders.

This stands in for the many situations in which the deep design of ubiquitous systems will shape the choices available to us in day-to-day life, in ways both subtle and less so. It's easy to imagine being denied access to some accommodation, for example, because of some machine-rendered judgment as to our suitability—and given a robustly interconnected everyware, that judgment may well hinge on something we did far away in both space and time from the scene of the exclusion.

Of course, we may never know just what triggered such events. In the case of our inherent attributes, maybe it's nothing we "did" at all. All we'll be able to guess is that we conformed to some profile, or violated the nominal contours of some other.

One immediate objection is that no sane society would knowingly deploy something like this—and we'll accept this point of view for the sake of argument, although again history gives us plenty of room for doubt. But what if segregation and similar unpleasant outcomes are "merely" an unintended consequence of unrelated, technical decisions? Once a technical system is in place, it has its own logic and momentum; as we've seen, the things that can be done with such systems, especially when interconnected, often have little to do with anything the makers imagined.*

We can only hope that those engineering ubiquitous systems weigh their decisions with the same consciousness of repercussion reflected in the design of the original Internet protocols. The downstream consequences of even the least significant-seeming architectural decision could turn out to be considerable—and unpleasant.

---

*As security expert Bruce Schneier says, "I think [a vendor of RFID security systems] understands this, and is encouraging use of its card everywhere: at sports arenas, power plants, even office buildings. This is just the sort of mission creep that moves us ever closer to a 'show me your papers' society."

Thesis 43

Everyware produces a wide belt of circumstances where human agency, judgment, and will are progressively supplanted by compliance with external, frequently algorithmically-applied, standards and norms.

One of the most attractive prospects of an ambient informatics is that information itself becomes freely available, at any place and any time. We can almost literally pull facts right out of the air, as and when needed, performing feats of knowledge and recall that people of any other era would rightly have regarded as prodigious.

But we're also likely to trade away some things we already know how to do. As Marshall McLuhan taught us, in his 1964 *Understanding Media*, "every extension is [also] an amputation." By this he meant that when we rely on technical systems to ameliorate the burdens of everyday life, we invariably allow our organic faculties to atrophy to a corresponding degree.

The faculty in question begins to erode, in a kind of willed surrender. Elevators allow us to live and work hundreds of feet into the air, but we can no longer climb even a few flights without becoming winded. Cars extend the radius of our travels by many times, but it becomes automatic to hop into one if we're planning to travel any further than the corner store—so much so that entire subdivisions are built around such assumptions, and once again we find behavior constrained at the level of architecture.

An example that may be more relevant to our present inquiry concerns phone numbers. Before speed dial, before mobile phones, you committed to memory the numbers of those closest to you. Now such mnemotechnical systems permit us to store these numbers in memory—an extension that, it is undeniable, allows us to retain many more numbers than would otherwise have been the case. But if I ask you your best friend's phone number? Or that of the local pizza place?

This is one danger of coming to rely too heavily, or too intimately, on ubiquitous technology. But unlike literal amputations, which tend to be pretty noticeable, these things only become visible in the default of the technical system in question. The consequences of an overreliance on extensions can clearly be seen in the aftermath of Hurricane Katrina, in which we saw that New Orleans' evacuation plan was predicated on the automobility of the city's entire population. When the storm revealed that assumption to have been unjustified, to say the least, we saw the stunning force with which a previously obscured amputation can suddenly breach the surface of awareness. McLuhan saw an uneasy, subliminal consciousness of what has been traded away at the root of the "never-explained numbness that each extension brings about in the individual and society."

"Amputation," though, implies that a faculty had at least once existed. But it's also the case that the presence of an ambient informatics might interfere in learning certain skills to begin with. Before I learned to drive, for example, I couldn't have given you any but the vaguest sort of directions. It wasn't until I acquired the fused haptic and cognitive experience of driving from origin to destination—the memory of making the decision to turn *here*, in other words, fused to the feeling of turning the wheel to make it so, and the perception of the consequences—that I laid down a mental map of the world in sufficient detail to permit me to convey that information to anyone else.

Children who grow up using everyware, told always where they are and how to get where they are going, may never acquire the same fluency. Able to rely on paraphernalia like personal location icons, route designators, and turn indicators, whether they will ever learn the rudiments of navigation—either by algorithm or by landmark or by dead reckoning—is open to question. Even memorizing street names might prove to be an amusingly antiquated demonstration of pointless skill, like knowing the number of pecks in a bushel.

If a reliance on ubiquitous systems robs us of some of our faculties, it may also cause us to lose faith in the ones that remain. We will find that everyware is subtly normative, even prescriptive—and, again, this will be something that is engineered into it at a deep level.

Take voice-recognition interfaces, for example. Any such system, no matter how sophisticated, will inscribe notions of a nominal voice profile that a speaker must match in order for his or her utterances to be recognized. Spoken commands made around a mouthful of coffee—or with a strong accent—may not be understood. It may turn out that ubiquitous voice recognition has more power to enforce crisp enunciation than any locution teacher ever dreamed of wielding.

This is problematic in two ways. First, of course, is the pragmatic concern that it forces users to focus on tool and not task, and thus violates every principle of an encalming pervasive technology. But more seriously, we probably weren't looking to our household management system for speech lessons. Why should we mold something as intimate, and as constitutive of personality, as the way we speak around some normative profile encoded into the systems around us?

There are still more insidious ways in which we can feel pressured to conform to technically-derived models of behavior. Some of the most unsettling are presented by biometric monitors such as BodyMedia's SenseWear patch.

BodyMedia's aim, as a corporate tagline suggests, is to "collect, process, and present" biometric information, with the strong implication that the information can and will be acted upon. This is, no doubt, a potential boon to millions of the sick, the infirm and the "worried well." But it's also a notion with other reverberations in a society that, at least for the moment, seems hell-bent on holding its members to ever-stricter ideals of form and fitness. For many of us, a product that retrieves biometric data painlessly, coupled to sophisticated visualization software that makes such data not merely visible but readily actionable, is going to be irresistible.

Notice how readily the conversation tends to drift onto technical grounds, though. Simply as a consequence of having the necessary tools available, we've begun to recast the body as a source of data rather than the seat of identity (let alone the soul). The problems therefore become ones of ensuring capture fidelity or interpreting the result, and not, say, how it feels to know that your blood pressure spikes whenever your spouse gets home from work. We forget to ask ourselves whether we feel OK about the way we look; we learn to override the wisdom and perspective that might counsel us that the danger posed by an occasional bacchanal is insignificant. We only notice how far our blood glucose levels have departed from the normative curve over the last 48 hours.

This is not to park such issues at BodyMedia's door alone. The same concerns could of course be raised about all of the systems increasingly deployed throughout our lives. The more deeply these systems infiltrate the decisions we make every day, the more they appear to call on all the powers of insight and inference implied by a relational technology, the less we may come to trust the evidence of our own senses.

Thesis 44

In the event of a default, fixing a locus of control may be effectively impossible.

Largely as a consequence of their complex and densely interwoven nature, in the event of a breakdown in ubiquitous systems, it may not be possible to figure out where something's gone wrong. Even expert technicians may find themselves unable to determine which component or subsystem is responsible for the default.

Let's consider the example of a "smart" household-management system, to which all of the local heating, lighting, ventilation, and plumbing infrastructure has been coupled. In the hope of striking a balance between comfort and economy, you've set its winter mode to lower any room's temperature to 60 degrees Fahrenheit when that room has been empty for ten minutes or more, but to maintain it at 68 otherwise.

When the heat fails to come on in one room or another, which of the interlinked systems involved has broken down? Is it a purely mechanical problem with the heater itself, the kind of thing you'd call a plumber for? Is it a hardware issue—say, a failure of the room's motion detector to properly register your presence? Maybe the management interface has locked up or crashed entirely. It's always possible that your settings file has become corrupt. Or perhaps these systems have between them gotten into some kind of strange feedback loop.

In the latter case particularly—where the problem may indeed not reside in any one place at all, but rather arises out of the complex interaction of independent parts—resolving the issue is going to present unusual difficulties. Diagnosis of simple defaults in ubiquitous systems will likely prove to be inordinately time-consuming by current standards, but systems that display emergent behavior may confound diagnosis entirely. Literally the only solution may be to power everything down and restart components one by one, in various combinations, until a workable and stable configuration is once again reached.

This will mean rebooting the car, or the kitchen, or your favorite sweater, maybe once and maybe several times, until every system that needs to do so has recognized the others and basic functionality has been restored to them all. And even then, of course, the interaction of their normal functioning may entrain the same breakdown. Especially when you consider how dependent on everyware we are likely to become, the prospect of having to cut through such a Gordian tangle of interconnected parts just to figure out which one has broken down is somewhat less than charming.

Thesis 45

Users will understand their transactions with everyware to be essentially social in nature.

There's good reason to believe that users will understand their transactions with ubiquitous systems to be essentially social in nature, whether consciously or otherwise—and this will be true even if there is only one human party to a given interaction.

Norbert Wiener, the "father of cybernetics," had already intuited something of this in his 1950 book, *The Human Use of Human Beings*: according to Wiener, when confronted with cybernetic machines, human beings found themselves behaving as if the systems possessed agency.

This early insight was confirmed and extended in the pioneering work of Byron Reeves and Clifford Nass, published in 1996 as *The Media Equation*. In an extensive series of studies, Reeves and Nass found that people treat computers more like other people than like anything else—that, in their words, computers "are *close enough* to human that they encourage *social* responses." (The emphasis is present in the original.) We'll flatter a computer, or try wheedling it into doing something we want, or insult it when it doesn't—even if, intellectually, we're perfectly aware how absurd this all is.

We also seem to have an easier time dealing with computers when they, in turn, treat us politely—when they apologize for interrupting our workflow or otherwise acknowledge the back-and-forth nature of communication in ways similar to those our human interlocutors might use. Reeves and Nass urge the designers of technical systems, therefore, to attend closely to the lessons we all learned in kindergarten and engineer their creations to observe at least the rudiments of interpersonal etiquette.

Past attempts to incorporate these findings into the design of technical systems, while invariably well-intentioned, have been disappointing. From Clippy, Microsoft's widely-loathed "Office Assistant" ("It looks like you're writing a letter"), to the screens of Japan Railways' ticket machines, which display an animated hostess bowing to the purchaser at the completion of each transaction, none of the various social interfaces have succeeded in doing anything more than reminding users of just how stilted and artificial the interaction is. Even Citibank's ATMs merely sound disconcerting, like some miserly cousin of HAL 9000, when they use the first person in apologizing for downtime or other violations of user expectations ("I'm sorry—I can only dispense cash in multiples of $20 right now.")

But genuinely internalizing the *Media Equation* insights will be critical for the designers of ubiquitous systems. Some are directly relevant to the attempted evocation of seamlessness ("Rule: Users will respond to the same voice on different computers as if it were the same social actor"), while others speak to the role of affect in the ubiquitous experience— notably, the authors' finding that the timing of interactions plays a critical role in shaping their interpretations, just as much as their content does.* Coming to grips with what Reeves and Nass are trying to tell us will help designers accept the notion that people will more often understand their interactions with everyware to be interpersonal in nature than technical.

These findings take on new importance when people encounter a technology that, by design, borders on the imperceptible. When there are fewer visible cues as to a system's exact nature, we're even more likely to mistake it for something capable of reciprocating our feelings—and we will be that much more hurt if it does not.

The example Reeves and Nass offer is how we react when praise is delayed by a critical few beats in response to a query—i.e., not well.

Thesis 46

Users will tend to blame themselves for defaults in everyware.

When ubiquitous systems break down, as they surely must from time to time, how will we react?

We've seen that it may be difficult to determine the origin of a problem, given a densely interwoven mesh of systems both local and remote—that emergent behavior arising in such a mesh means that there mightn't even be a single point of failure, in the classical sense.

We've also seen that users are likely to understand their interactions with everyware as primarily social in nature. Reeves and Nass tell us, further, that we generally treat informatic systems as though they had personalities, complete with agency—in other words, that we'll routinely fail to see through a system to the choices of its designers. As a consequence, we show a marked reluctance to ascribe blame to the systems themselves when things go wrong: we don't want to hurt their feelings (!). Even in the depths of this narcissistic age, we're still, apparently, gracious and forgiving in our dealings with information technology.

Given these two boundary constraints, the most obvious option remaining open is for users to blame themselves. We can expect that this will in fact be the most frequent user response to defaults in the ubiquitous and pervasive systems around them.

I can only cite my own experiences in support of this idea. As an information architect and user-experience consultant, I've helped to develop more than fifty enterprise-scale Web sites over the last seven years, as well as a smaller number of kiosk-based and mobile-phone interfaces. My work frequently involves the assessment of a client's existing site—

observing real users in their interactions with it and attending closely to their subjective responses. And one thing that I've seen with a fair, if disheartening, degree of regularity in this work is that users blame themselves when they can't get a site to work properly—and this is more true the less technically sophisticated the user is.

This very much despite the fact that the site in question may simply be wretchedly designed. People will say "I can't figure this out," "I'm too stupid," or "I get confused so easily," far more often than they'll venture an opinion that the site's designers or developers have done an incompetent job. Especially as everyware subtends an ever-larger population of nonspecialists—everyday people without any particular interest in the workings of the information technology they rely on—we can expect to see similar responses grow more and more common in reaction to breakdowns and defaults.

And this is the ultimate "next larger context" for our considerations of everyware. If we wish to design ubiquitous systems to support people in all the richness and idiosyncrasy of their lives, that address the complications of those lives without introducing new ones, we should bear in mind how crushingly often our mistakes will come to haunt not us but the people on whose behalf we're supposed to be acting.

But who, really, is this mysterious "we" I keep talking about? Up until this point, I've spoken as though responsibility for determining the shape of the ubiquitous future is general in the world and in the audience for these words as well—but surely not everyone reading this book will be able to exert an identical amount of influence on that shape. As we head into the next section, then, we'll consider these questions with a greater degree of rigor: Who gets to speak for users? And just who will decide what kind of everyware we're to be furnished with?

Who gets to determine the shape of everyware?

Beyond the purely technical, there are powerful social, cultural, and economic forces that will act as boundary constraints on the kind of everyware that comes into being. What are these forces? What sorts of influences will they bring to bear on the ubiquitous technology we encounter in daily life? And especially, who has the power to decide these issues?

Thesis 47

The practice of technological development is tending to become more decentralized.

Sometime in early 2002—in an agnès b. store in Shibuya, of all places—I heard the full-throated sound of the new century for the first time. The track thumping from the store's sound system bent the familiar surge of Iggy and the Stooges' "No Fun" to the insistent beat of "Push It" by Salt'n'Pepa, and it was just as the old commercials promised: These truly were two great tastes that tasted great together. Rarely, in fact, had any music sent such an instant thrill of glee and profound *rightness* through me. The next track smashed the Velvet Underground classic "I'm Waiting For The Man" into some gormless eighties hit, and that was almost as tasty; I found myself literally pogo-dancing around the store.

I had caught the mashup virus. A mashup is just about what it sounds like: the result of a DJ taking two unrelated songs and—by speeding, slowing, or otherwise manipulating one or both of them—hybridizing them into something entirely new. Anyone can do it, really, but the genius of a truly clever mashup is finding some note of deep complementarity in two source texts that seemingly could not possibly have less to do with one another. After all, until this particular gang of provocateurs—a Belgian duo calling themselves 2 Many DJs—came along, who ever would have thought that a prime slab of Motor City protopunk circa 1969 would have worked so well against a sassily righteous hip-hop single of the mid-1980s?

I was hooked, all right. What I didn't understand at the time, though, was that I had also been given a first glimpse of one of the most important ideas to hit software development since object-oriented programming achieved widespread acceptance in the mid-1980s. The cultural logic of the mashup, in which amateurs pick up pieces already at hand

and plug them into each other in unexpected and interesting ways, turns out to be perfectly suited to an age of open and distributed computational resources—the "small pieces loosely joined" that make up the contemporary World Wide Web, in essayist David Weinberger's evocative phrasing.

In the case of the Web, the ingredients of a mashup are not songs, but services provided by sites such as Google and Yahoo! and the community site Craigslist, each of which generates enormous quantities of data on a daily basis. Services like these have at their core an extensive database that is more or less richly tagged with *metadata*—information about information, such as where and when a picture was taken, or the ZIP code of an apartment listing. When millions of pieces of such self-describing data are made available—tossed on the table like so many Lego bricks, as it were—it's easy for third-party applications to pick them up and plug them into one another.

And so we see mashups from HousingMaps, which combines apartment listings from Craigslist with Google Maps to produce a searchable map of available rentals, to Stamen Design's Mappr, which uses metadata associated with images drawn from the Flickr photo-sharing service to plot them on a map of the United States. There's even a free application called Ning that lets anyone build a custom mashup, employing what might be called the Chinese menu approach: choose an application from Column A, another from Column B, and so on. It is simultaneously a profound demystification of the development process and a kit of parts that lets people without any programming experience to speak of build local, small-scale applications perfectly tuned to their specific needs.

What does any of this have to do with everyware? It suggests that we're about to experience a significant and unprecedented growth in the number of nonspecialists empowered to develop homebrew applications. It's crucial that the tools exist that allow us to do so, but still more important is a cultural context that not merely permits but encourages us to experiment—and that is just what the sense of ferment around mashups provides us.

Especially when combined with the revolution in conceptions of intellectual property that was originally sparked by the open-source and free software movements, we have everything necessary to democratize the development of information technology. What was not so very long ago a matter of a few thousand corporate and academic research centers will explode to encompass tens or even hundreds of millions of independent, unaffiliated developers scattered across the globe.

As a result, everyware is not going to be something simply vended to a passive audience by the likes of Intel and Samsung: What tools such as Ning tell us is that there will be millions of homebrew designer/makers developing their own modules of functionality, each of which will bear the hooks that allow it to be plugged into others.

Of course, not everyone will be interested in becoming a developer: The far greater proportion of people will continue to be involved with information technology primarily as users and consumers. And for the time being, anyway, the sheer complexity of ubiquitous systems will mitigate the otherwise strong turn toward amateurism that has characterized recent software development. But over the longer term, the centrifugal trend will be irresistible. The practice of technological development itself will become decisively decentralized, in a way that hasn't been true for at least a century.

Thesis 48

Those developing everyware may have little idea that this is in fact what they are doing.

Given how conventional a component system may appear before it is incorporated in some context we'd be able to recognize as everyware, we're led to a rather startling conclusion: Relatively few of the people engaged in developing the building blocks of ubiquitous systems will consciously think of what they're doing as such.

In fact, they may never have heard the phrase "ubiquitous computing" or any of its various cognates. They will be working, rather, on finer-grained problems: calibrating the sensitivity of a household sensor grid so that it recognizes human occupants but not the cat, or designing an RFID-equipped key fob so that it reads properly no matter which of its surfaces is brought into range of the reader. With such a tight focus, they will likely have little sense for the larger schemes into which their creations will fit.

This is not an indictment of engineers. They are given a narrow technical brief, and they return solutions within the envelope available to them—an envelope that is already bounded by material, economic, and time constraints. Generally speaking, it is not in their mandate to consider the "next larger context" of their work.

And if this is true of professional engineers, how much more so will it apply to all the amateurs newly empowered to develop alongside them? Amateurs have needs and desires, not mandates. They'll build tools to address the problem at hand, and inevitably some of these tools will fall under the rubric of everyware—but the amateur developers will be highly unlikely to think of what they are doing in these terms.

Thesis 49

Present IT development practices as applied to everyware will result in unacceptably bad user experience.

In Weiser and Brown's seminal "The Coming Age of Calm Technology," it appears to have been the authors' contention that responses to a suddenly hegemonic computing would arise as a consequence of its very ubiquity: "If computers are everywhere, they better stay out of the way."

Given the topic, this is a strikingly passive way for them to frame the question. It's as if Weiser and Brown trusted all of the people developing ubiquitous technology to recognize the less salutary implications of their efforts ahead of time and plan accordingly.

Even in the pre-Web 1990s, this was an unreasonably optimistic stance—and taking into account all that we've concluded about how little developers may understand the larger context in which their work is embedded, and the difficulty of planning for emergent properties of interacting systems, it would be indefensible today.

In fact, we should probably regard IT development itself as something unsuited to the production of an acceptably humane everyware. The reason has to do with how such development is conducted in organizations both large and small, from lean and hungry startups to gigantic international consultancies.

Every developer is familiar with the so-called "iron triangle." The version I learned was taught to me by a stereotypically crusty engineer, way back at my first dot-com job in 1999. In response to my request that he build a conduit between our Web site's shopping cart and the warehouse's inventory control system, he grunted, scrawled a quick triangle up on a handy whiteboard, hastily labeled the vertices FAST, GOOD, and CHEAP, and said, "Pick any two."

For all that this is obviously a cartoon of the technology development process, it's also an accurate one. For a variety of reasons, from the advantages that ostensibly accrue to first movers to the constraints imposed by venture capitalists, shareholders, and other bottom-liners, GOOD is rarely among the options pursued. Given the inherent pressures of the situation, it often takes an unusually dedicated, persistent, and powerful advocate—Steve Jobs comes to mind, as does vacuum-cleaner entrepreneur James Dyson—to see a high-quality design project through to completion with everything that makes it excellent intact.

Moreover, the more complex the product or service at hand, the more likely it will be to have a misguided process of "value engineering" applied at some point between inception and delivery. Although the practice has its roots in an entirely legitimate desire to prune away redundancy and overdesign, it is disastrous when applied to IT development. However vital, the painstakingly detailed work of ensuring a good user experience is frequently hard to justify on a short-term ROI basis, and this is why it is often one of the first things to get value-engineered out of an extended development process. Even if it's clearly a false efficiency from a more strategic perspective, reducing or even eliminating the user-experience phase of development can seem like getting rid of an unnecessary complication.

But we've seen that getting everyware right will be orders of magnitude more complicated than achieving acceptable quality in a Web site, let alone a desktop application. We have an idea how very difficult it will be to consistently produce ubiquitous experiences that support us, encalm us, strengthen and encourage us. Where everyware is concerned, even GOOD won't be GOOD enough. This is not the place for value engineers, not unless they have first earned a sensitive understanding of how difficult the problem domain is and what kinds of complexity it genuinely requires— both in process and product.

Thesis 50

Everyware will appear differently in different places: that is, there is and will be no one continuum of adoption.

Remember our first thesis, that there are many ubiquitous computings? This is never truer than in the sense that everyware will prove to be different, in fundamental and important ways, in every separate cultural context in which it appears. In fact, the most basic assumptions as to what constitutes ubiquitous computing can differ from place to place.

An old Taoist proverb asks whether it is wiser to pave the world in soft leather or simply find yourself a nice comfortable pair of shoes. Along similar lines, some question the wisdom of any attempt to instrument the wider world. Such unwieldy "infrastructural" approaches, they argue, amount to overkill, when all that is really desired is that people have access to services wherever they happen to go.

One such perspective is offered by Teruyasu Murakami, head of research for Nomura Research Institute and author of a doctrine Nomura calls the "ubiquitous network paradigm." In Murakami's view, the mobile phone or its immediate descendent, the Ubiquitous Communicator, will do splendidly as a mediating artifact for the delivery of services.* His point: is it really necessary to make the heavy investment required for an

---

Contemporary Japanese ubicomp schemes often specify the use of such "Ubiquitous Communicators" or "UCs." While the form factors and capabilities of UCs are rarely specified in detail, it can be assumed that they will follow closely on the model offered by current-generation keitai, or mobile phones.

infrastructural approach to the delivery of services if people can take the network with them?

Taking the present ubiquity of PDAs, smartphones, and mobiles as a point of departure, scenarios like Murakami's—similar schemes have in the past been promoted by the likes of Nokia and the old AT&T—imagine that the widest possible range of daily tasks will be mediated by a single device, the long-awaited "remote control for your life." If you live outside one of the places on Earth where mobile phone usage is all but universal, this may sound a little strange to you, but it happens to be a perfectly reasonable point of view (with the usual reservations) if you live in Japan.*

In the West, the development of everyware has largely proceeded along classically Weiserian lines, with the project understood very much as an infrastructural undertaking. In Japan, as has been the case so often in the past, evolution took a different fork, resulting in what the cultural anthropologist Mizuko Ito has referred to as an "alternatively technologized modernity."

With adoption rates for domestic broadband service lagging behind other advanced consumer cultures—North America, Western Europe, Korea—and a proportionally more elaborate culture emerging around *keitai,* it didn't make much sense for Japan to tread quite the same path to everyware as other places. The Web per se has never met with quite the same acceptance here as elsewhere; by contrast, mobile phones are inescapable, and the range of what people use them for is considerably broader. Many things North Americans or Europeans might choose to do via the Web—buy movie tickets, download music, IM a friend—are accomplished locally via the mobile Internet.

Ito argues that "the Japan mobile Internet case represents a counterweight to the notion that PC-based broadband is the current apex of

---

The reservations are both practical and philosophical: What happens if you lose your Ubiquitous Communicator, or leave it at home? But also: Why should people have to subscribe to phone services if all they want is to avail themselves of pervasive functionality?

Internet access models; characteristics such as ubiquity, portability, and lightweight engagement form an alternative constellation of 'advanced' Internet access characteristics that contrast to complex functionality and stationary immersive engagement."

Indeed, in the words of a 2005 design competition sponsored by Japanese mobile market leader NTT DoCoMo, the mobile phone "has become an indispensable tool for constructing the infrastructure of everyday life." Despite the rather self-serving nature of this proposition, and its prima facie falsehood in the context of Western culture, it's probably something close to the truth in Japanese terms. This is a country where, more so than just about anywhere else, people plan gatherings, devise optimal commutes, and are advised of the closest retailers via the intercession of their phones.

Given the facts on the ground, Japanese developers wisely decided to concentrate on the ubiquitous delivery of services via *keitai*—for example, the RFID-tagged streetlamps of Shinjuku already discussed, or the QR codes we'll be getting to shortly. And as both phones themselves and the array of services available for them become more useful and easier to use, we approach something recognizable as the threshold of everyware. This is a culture that has already made the transition to a regime of ambient informatics—as long, that is, as you have a phone. As a result, it's a safe bet to predict that the greater part of Japanese efforts at designing everyware will follow the mobile model for the foreseeable future.

Rather than casting this as an example of how Japanese phone culture is "more advanced" than North America's, or, conversely, evidence that Japan "doesn't get the Web" (the latter a position I myself have been guilty of taking in the past), it is simply the case that different pressures are operating in these two advanced technological cultures—different tariffs on voice as opposed to data traffic, different loci of control over pricing structures, different physical circumstances resulting in different kinds of legacy networks, different notions about monopoly and price-fixing—and they've predictably produced characteristically different effects. This will be true of every local context in which ideas about ubiquitous computing appear.

Many of the boundary conditions around the development of everyware will be sociocultural in nature. For example, one point of view I've heard expressed in the discussion around contemporary Korean ubicomp projects is that East Asians, as a consequence of the Confucian values their societies are at least nominally founded on, are more fatalistic about issues of privacy than Westerners would be in similar circumstances. I'm not at all sure I buy this myself, but the underlying point is sound: Different initial conditions of culture will reliably produce divergent everywares.

Is there more than one pathway to everyware? Absolutely. Individuals make choices about technology all the time, and societies do as well. I won't have a video game in the house—the last thing I need is another excuse to burn life time; I've never particularly warmed to fax machines; and I do not and will not do SMS. On a very different level, the governments of Saudi Arabia and the People's Republic of China have clearly decided that the full-on clamor of the Internet is not for them—or, more properly, not for their citizens. So the nature and potential of technology only go so far in determining what is made of it. The truly vexing challenge will reside in deciding what kind of everyware is right for this place, at this time, under these circumstances.

Thesis 51

The precise shape of everyware is contingent on the decisions made by designers, regulators, and markets of empowered buyers. The greater mass of people exposed to such systems are likely to have relatively little say in their composition.

If societies are afforded some leeway in choosing just how a particular technology appears, what does history tell us about how this process has played out in the recent past?

Societies, as it happens, turn their backs on technologies all the time, even some that seem to be at the very cusp of their accession to prominence. Citizen initiatives have significantly shaped the emergence—and the commercial viability—of biotechnology and genetically modified foods planetwide; concerns both ethical and environmental continue to be raised about cloning and nanotechnology.* Nor are Americans any exception to the general rule, however happy we are to be seen (and to portray ourselves) as a nation of can-do techno-optimists: In the past twenty years, we've rejected fission power and supersonic commercial aviation, to name just two technologies that once seemed inevitable. And these outcomes, too, had a lot to do with local struggles and grassroots action.

Some would say that bottom-up resistance to such technologies arises out of an almost innumerate inability to calculate risk—out of simple

---

For that matter, similar concerns have also been raised about producing computing on a scale sufficient to supply the rural developing world with "$100 laptops." See, e.g., worldchanging.com.

fear of the unknown, that is, rather than any reasoned cost-benefit analysis. There are also, without doubt, those who feel that such resistance "impedes progress." But outcomes such as these stand as testament to a certain vigor remaining in democracy: In considering the debates over fission and the SST, the clear lesson—as corny as it may seem—is that the individual voice has made a difference. And this has been the case even when groups of disconnected individuals have faced coherent, swaggeringly self-confident, and infinitely better-funded pro-technology lobbies.

So on the one hand, we have reason to trust that "the system works." At least in the United States, we have some reason to believe that the ordinary messy process of democracy functions effectively to discover those technologies whose adoption appears particularly unwise, even if it's not necessarily able to propose meaningful alternatives to them. And this may well turn out to be the case where the more deleterious aspects of ubiquitous technology are concerned.

But something tells me everyware will be different. It's a minuscule technology, one that proceeds by moments and levers its way in via whatever crevices it is afforded. It will call itself by different names, it will appear differently from one context to another, and it will almost always wear the appealing masks of safety or convenience. And as we've seen, the relevant choices will be made by a relatively large number of people each responding to their own local need—"large," anyway, as compared to the compact decision nexus involved in the production of a fission plant or a supersonic airliner.

Who, then, will get to determine the shape of the ubiquitous computing we experience?

Designers, obviously—by which I mean the entire apparatus of information-technology production, from initial conceptual framing straight through to marketing.

Regulators, too, will play a part; given everyware's clear potential to erode privacy, condition public space, and otherwise impinge on the exercise of civil liberties, there is a legitimate role for state actors here.

And markets surely will. In fact, of all of these influences, the market is likely to have the most significant impact on what kinds of everyware find their way into daily use, with self-evidently dangerous, wasteful, or pointless implementations facing the usual penalties. But let's not get carried away with enthusiasm about the power of markets to converge on wise choices—as anyone who's been involved with technology can tell you, buyers are frequently not at all the same people as end users, and there are many instances in which their interests are diametrically opposed to one another. A corporate IT department, for example, generally purchases PCs based on low bid, occasionally ease of maintenance; the user experience is rarely factored, as it properly should be, into estimates of the total cost of ownership (TCO).

Left out of these considerations, though, is the greater mass of people who will be affected by the appearance of everyware, who will find their realities shaped in countless ways by the advent of a pervasive, ubiquitous, and ambient informatics. And while there is a broad community of professionals—usability specialists, interaction designers, information architects, and others working under the umbrella of user experience—that has been able to advocate for the end user in the past, with varying degrees of effectiveness, that community's practice is still oriented primarily to the challenges of personal computing. The skill sets and especially the mindsets appropriate to user-experience work in everyware have barely begun to be developed.

This raises the crucial question of timing. Are discussions of everyware abstract debates best suited to the coffeehouse and the dorm room, or are they items for near-term agendas, things we should be discussing in our school-board and city-council and shareholder meetings right now?

I strongly believe that the latter is true—that the interlocking influences of designer, regulator, and market will be most likely to result in beneficial outcomes if these parties all treat everyware as a present reality, and if the decision makers concerned act accordingly. This is especially true of members of the user experience community, who will best be able to intervene effectively if they develop appropriate insights, tools, and methodologies ahead of the actual deployment of ubiquitous systems.

In Section 6 we will consider why—while everyware is indeed both an immediate issue and a "hundred-year problem"—it makes the most sense to treat everyware as an emergent reality in the near term.

When do we need to begin preparing for everyware?

We've gotten a sense of the various factors shaping the development of ubiquitous computing—and of the different forms that computing will take in different places.

Which of the many challenges involved in bringing it into being have been resolved? And which remain to be addressed? Most important, how much time do we have to prepare for the actuality of everyware?

Thesis 52

At most, everyware will subsume traditional computing paradigms. It will not supplant them—certainly not in the near term.

In determining when everyware might realistically arrive, the first notion that we need to dispense with is that it is an all-or-nothing proposition. Just as there are still mainframes and minicomputers chugging away in the world, doing useful work unthreatened by the emergence of the PC, the advent of ubiquitous computing will not mean the disappearance of earlier forms.

Wearables, embedded sensors, RFID-based infrastructures of one sort or another, and the many other systems that we've here defined as ubiquitous in nature can—in fact already do—happily coexist with thoroughly ordinary desktops and laptops. Even after information processing begins to pervade the environment in more decisive ways, there will continue to be a healthy measure of backward compatibility; for some time yet to come, anyone writing a dissertation, keeping a budget, or designing a logo will be likely to interact with conventional applications running on relatively conventional machines.

Personal computers of relatively familiar aspect will continue to be made and sold for the foreseeable future, though they will increasingly tend to be conceived of as portals onto the far greater functionality offered by the local constellation of ubiquitous resources. Such PCs may well serve as the hub by which we access and control the mélange of technical systems imperceptibly deployed everywhere around us, without ever quite disappearing themselves. We could say the same of the various "Ubiquitous Communicator"-style phones that have been proposed, in that they'll persist as discrete objects very much at the focus of attention.

It's true that this kind of setup doesn't go terribly far toward fulfilling Weiser and Brown's hopes for a calm technology, but neither is it quite what we've thought of as personal computing historically. Such scenarios illustrate the difficulties of inscribing a hard-and-fast line between the two paradigms, let alone specifying a date by which personal computing will indisputably have disappeared from the world. Moreover, there will always be those, whatever their motivation, who prefer to maintain independent, stand-alone devices—and if for no other reason than this, the personal computer is likely to retain a constituency for many years past its "sell-by" date.

The safest conclusion to draw is that, while there will continue to be room for PCs in the world, this should not be construed as an argument against the emergence of a more robust everyware. If the border between personal and ubiquitous computing is not always as clear as we might like, that should not be taken as an admission that the latter will not turn out to have enormous consequences for all of us.

Thesis 53

Depending on how it is defined, everyware is both an immediate issue and a "hundred-year problem."

The question of how soon we need to begin preparing for everyware really turns on how strictly it is defined. If we're simply using the word to denote artifacts like PayPass cards and Smart Hydro bathtubs, then it's clear that "preparing" is out of the question: these things already exist.

But everyware is also, and simultaneously, what HP Laboratories' Gene Becker calls a "hundred-year problem": a technical, social, ethical and political challenge of extraordinary subtlety and difficulty, resistant to comprehensive solution in anything like the near term. In fact, if we use the word "everyware" maximally, to mean a seamless and intangible application of information processing that causes change to occur, whether locally or remotely, in perfect conformity with the user's will, we may never quite get there however hard we try.

As is so often the case, the useful definition will be found somewhere in between these two extremes. The trouble is that we're not particularly likely to agree on just *where* in between: we've already seen that there are many ubiquitous computings, and as if that weren't complication enough, we've also seen that there are places where the line between personal and ubiquitous computing is fairly blurry to begin with.

So how are we to arrive at an answer to our question? Let's see whether we can't narrow the window of possible responses somewhat, by considering schematically which of the components required by a truly ubiquitous computing are already in place and which remain to be developed.

Many such components already exist in forms capable of underwriting a robust everyware, even in the scenarios imagined by its more exuberant proponents. And while a very high degree of finesse in implementation is an absolute precondition for any sort of acceptable user experience, there's nothing in principle that keeps these components from being used to build ubiquitous applications today:

- Processor speeds are sufficient to all but the most computationally intensive tasks.
- Storage devices offer the necessary capacity.
- Displays have the necessary flexibility, luminance and resolution.
- The necessary bridges between the physical reality of atoms and the information space of bits exist.
- The necessary standards for the representation and communication of structured data exist.
- A sufficiently capacious addressing scheme exists.

What makes a system composed of these elements "ubiquitous" in the first place is the fact that its various organelles need not be physically coextensive; given the right kind of networking protocol, they can be distributed as necessary throughout local reality. As it happens, an appropriate protocol exists, and so we can add this too to the list of things that need not hold us back.

But there are also a few limiting factors we may wish to consider. These are the circumstances that have thus far tended to inhibit the appearance of everyware, and which will continue to do so until addressed decisively:

- Broad standards for the interoperability of heterogeneous devices and interfaces do not exist.
- In most places, the deployed networking infrastructure is insufficient to support ubiquitous applications.
- Appropriate design documents and conventions simply do not exist, nor is there a community consciously devoted to the design of ubiquitous systems at anything like industrial scale.
- There is barely any awareness on the part of users as to the existence of ubiquitous systems, let alone agreement as to their value or utility.

Overall, these issues are much less tractable than the purely technological challenges posed by processor speed or storage capacity, and it's these which account for much of the complexity implied by Becker's "hundred-year problem." We'll consider each point individually before venturing an answer as to when everyware will become an urgent reality.

My own contention is that, while the existence of this latter set of factors constitutes a critical brake on the longer-term development of everyware, the social and ethical questions I am most interested in are activated even by systems that are less total in ambition and extent—some of which are already deployed and fully operational. So we'll consider a few such operational systems as well. By the time the section concludes, I hope you will agree with me that however long it may take a full-fledged everyware to appear, the moment to begin developing a praxis appropriate to it is now.

Thesis 54

Many problems posed by everyware are highly resistant to comprehensive solution in the near term.

By now, the outlines of this thing we've been sketching are clear.

We've taken concepts originating in logistics, chip design, network theory, cultural anthropology, computer-supported collaborative work, and dozens of other disciplines, and fused them into a computing that has become genuinely ubiquitous in our lives, as present in our thoughts as it will be in our tools and jobs and cities.

Most of these "small pieces" are matters of the real world and the present day—a few, admittedly, only as incremental steps or standards adopted but not yet implemented. Even in many of the latter cases, though, we can reasonably expect that the necessary pieces of the puzzle will appear within the next year or two.

But even though we already have most of the componentry we'll ever require, there are excellent reasons to suppose that everyware will take decades to mature fully. Sprawling, amorphous, it touches on so many areas of our lives, complicates social and political debates that are already among the thorniest our societies have ever faced. In some cases, indeed, we may never fully master the challenges involved. The following are some of the factors that *are* actively inhibiting either the development or the chances for adoption of ubiquitous computing.

Thesis 55

The necessary standards for interoperability do not exist or are not yet widely observed.

A lack of widely observed standards in the dimensions of screw threading inhibited Charles Babbage in his quest to build the Difference Engine, the world's first computer, in the 1840s. A lack of standards in languages and operating systems kept electronic computers from communicating with each other for decades. Well into the era of the personal computer, a lack of standards kept software development balkanized. A lack of standards led to the so-called Browser Wars, which suppressed adoption of the World Wide Web straight into the early years of this decade, as institutions that wanted Web sites were forced to build different versions compatible with each browser then widely used.

This afflicts almost all technologies at some point during their evolution, not just computing. Every American owner of a VW Beetle remembers the hassle of driving a car engineered to metric tolerances in an English-measurement culture; to this day, travelers arriving by rail at the French-Spanish border are forced to change trains because the countries' standard track gauges differ. The matter of standards seems to be a place where we are always having to learn the same lesson.

In some cases, there's a reasonable excuse for one or another system's failure to observe the relevant convention; The Octopus smartcard scheme we'll be discussing, for example, uses an idiosyncratic RFID architecture that does not conform to the ISO 14443 standard, simply because it was first deployed before the standard itself was established.

In other cases, the thicket of incompatible would-be standards is a matter of jockeying for advantageous position in a market that has not yet fully matured. We see this in the wireless networking arena, for example, where it can be hard even for a fairly knowledgeable observer to disentangle the competing specifications, to distinguish Wireless USB from Wi-Media, next-generation Bluetooth, and IEEE 802.15.3a—or even to determine whether they compete on the same ground.

There are good commercial reasons for this, of course. Every manufacturer would ideally like to be able to benefit from the "lock-in" effect, in which its entry is recognized as the universal standard, as happened when JVC's VHS beat Sony's ostensibly superior Betamax format early in the adoption of home video. (It is a persistent urban legend that this was in large part due to Sony's refusal to license pornographic content for Betamax.) VHS, of course, went on to become a multibillion-dollar industry, while the Beta format was more or less forgotten, by all except a diehard few. Sony certainly remembers: It has absolutely no intention of letting its high-capacity Blu-Ray DVD format lose out to the competing HD DVD standard.

But what gets lost in the shuffle in such cases is that the jockeying can permanently retard adoption of a technology, especially when it goes on for long enough that the technology itself is leapfrogged. This was the case with early HDTV efforts: Competing producers advanced their incompatible analog standards for so long that a far superior digital HDTV technology emerged in the interim. None of the parties originally marketing analog standards are competitive in HDTV today.

Sometimes lock-in and other legacy issues inhibit the adoption of a standard that might otherwise seem ideal for a given application. We'll be seeing how powerful and general XML is where there is a requirement to communicate structured data between applications, but even given its clear suitability there are some prominent contexts in which it's not yet used. To take two familiar examples, neither the EXIF data that encodes properties such as date, time, and camera type in digital images, nor the ID3 tags that allow MP3 players to display metadata such as track, artist, and album name, are expressed in valid XML. And yet, as we'll be seeing, this is exactly the kind of application XML is well suited for. Whatever the reasons for maintaining separate formats, surely their advantages would be outweighed by those attending compliance with a more universal scheme?

Finally, even where broadly applicable technical standards exist, compliance with them is still subject to the usual vagaries—a process that can be seen, in microcosm, in the market for pet-identification RFID transponders.

The United Kingdom mandates that all pet transponders and veterinary readers sold conform to the ISO FDXB standard. A single countrywide registry called PetLog, maintained by the national Kennel Club and recognized by the government's Department for Food, Environment and Rural Affairs, contains some two million records, and lost pets are routinely reunited with their owners as a result of the system's deployment.

By contrast, in the United States, there is no national standard for such tags; your vet has whatever scanner system he or she happens to have bought, which can read the proprietary tags sold by the scanner manufacturer, but not others. Should your pet wander into the next town over and get taken to a vet or a pound using an RFID system from a different vendor, the odds of its being properly identified are slim indeed.

In this case, as in so many others, it's not that a relevant standard does not exist; it does, and it's evidently being used successfully elsewhere. It's merely a question of when, or whether, some combination of pressures from the bottom up (market incentives, consumer action) and the top down (regulation, legislation) will result in a convergence on one universal standard. And we understand by now, certainly, that such processes can drag on for an indefinite amount of time.

Thesis 56

The necessary network infrastructure does not exist.

Whether they themselves are infrastructural or mobile in nature, all of the visions of everyware we've considered in this book depend vitally on near-universal broadband network access.

And although it frequently seems that each day's newspaper brings word of another large-scale Internet access initiative—from Philadelphia's effort to provide a blanket of free municipal Wi-Fi to Google's similar endeavor on behalf of San Francisco—the network infrastructure so necessary to these visions simply does not exist yet in most places.

Even in the United States, broadband penetration is significantly less than total, and as of the end of 2005, many Internet users still eke by with dial-up connections. The problem is particularly exacerbated in areas far from the dense urban cores, where the possibility of ever being fully wired—let alone richly provided with overlapping areas of wireless service—is simply out of the question. Given the economics involved, even in an age of satellite broadband, it's been speculated that some analogue of the Tennessee Valley Authority's Rural Electrification Program of the 1930s might be necessary if universal high-speed connectivity is ever to be a reality.

Newer technologies like WiMAX, especially as used to support mesh networks, show every sign of addressing these issues, but we'll have to wait for their scheduled deployment during 2006-2007 to see whether they make good on the claims of their proponents. Unless these challenges can be resolved, all we'll ever be able to build is a computing that is indeed ubiquitous, but only in some places.

If this sounds like an absurdity, it isn't. Many of these places will be domains large enough for the bulk of our social and experiential concerns to come into play: corporate and university campuses, even entire cities. It may simply be some time before these concerns are fully relevant to the majority of people, even in the developed nations.

Finally, though raising this point may sound an odd note here, we should never forget that many human places abide without electricity, running water, or sewerage, let alone Internet access. As much as I believe that information is power, there's no question that shelter, safe drinking water and sanitation come first—on Maslow's pyramid and in any development scheme I'd want to endorse. Whatever promise everyware may extend to us, it will be quite some time indeed until we all get to share its benisons on anything like an equal footing.

Thesis 57

Appropriate design documents and conventions do not yet exist.

One unexpected factor that that may inhibit the development of everyware for some time to come is that, while the necessary technical underpinnings may exist, a robust design practice devoted to the field does not. As designers, we haven't even begun to agree on the conventions we'll use to describe the systems we intend to build.

Consider what is involved in an analogous process of development, the design of a large-scale Web site. The success of the whole effort hinges on the accurate communication of ideas among members of the development team. The person who actually has to code the site is joined by the visual designer, who is responsible for the graphic look and feel; the information architect, responsible for the structure and navigation; and perhaps a content strategist, who ensures that written copy and "navitorial" convey a consistent "tone and voice." When sites are developed by agencies operating on behalf of institutional clients, invariably there will also be input from a client-facing account manager as well as representatives of the client's own marketing or corporate communications department.

The documents that are used to coordinate the process among all the parties involved are referred to as "deliverables." A reasonably comprehensive set of deliverables for a Web site might include visual comps, which depict the graphic design direction; a site map, which establishes the overall structure of the site as well as specifying the navigational relationship of a given page to the others; schematics, which specify the navigational options and content available on a given page; and task flows and use cases, which depict trajectories through the site in highly granular detail.

All of these things are signed off on by the client, after which they are released to the software development engineer, who is then responsible for the actual coding of the site.

When done conscientiously, this is an involved, painstaking process, one that can go on for many months and cost hundreds of thousands of dollars. Success in the endeavor depends vitally on accurate deliverables that clearly convey what is required.

No such deliverables currently exist for everyware. If everyware presents situations in which multiple actors interact simultaneously with multiple systems in a given environment, in three dimensions of space and one of time, we lack the conventions that would allow us to represent such interactions to each other. If everyware implies that the state of remote systems may impinge quite profoundly on events unfolding here and now, we scarcely have a way to model these influences. If everyware involves mapping gesture to system behavior, we lack whatever equivalent of choreographic notation would be necessary to consistently describe gesture numerically. And where the Web, until very recently, was governed by a page metaphor that associated a consistent address with a known behavior, interaction in everyware lacks for any such capacity. As designers, we simply don't yet know how to discuss these issues—not with each other, not with our clients, and especially not with the people using the things we build.

At present, these challenges are resolved on a bespoke, case-by-case basis, and development teams have tended to be small and homogeneous enough that the necessary ideas can easily be conveyed, one way or another. This is strikingly reminiscent of design practice in the early days of the Web—a glorious moment in which a hundred flowers certainly bloomed, and yet so terribly disappointing in that ninety-six of them turned out to be weeds.

Just as was the case with the Web, as everyware matures—and especially as it becomes commercialized and diffuses further into the world—there will be a greater demand for consistency, reliability and accountability, and this will mandate the creation of deliverable formats to account for all of the relevant variables. It is true that such design documents did not exist for hypertext systems prior to the advent of the World Wide Web, and that a practice developed and to some degree became formalized within just a few years. Nevertheless, with regard to everyware, this conversation hasn't even properly started yet.

Thesis 58

As yet, everyware offers the user no compelling and clearly stated value proposition.

The last of the inhibiting factors we'll be discussing is the deep and as yet unaddressed disconnect that exists between the current discourse around ubiquitous systems, and any discernable desire on the part of meaningfully large populations for such systems.

Inside the field, however elaborated they've become with an embroidery of satisfying and clever details, we've told each other these tales of ubiquity so many times that they've become rote, even clichéd—but we've forgotten to ascertain whether or not they make any sense to anyone outside the contours of our consensual hallucination.

HP's Gene Becker describes the issue this way:

> The potential uses and benefits of ubicomp often seem 'obvious'; most of us in the field have spun variations of the same futuristic scenarios, to the point where it seems like a familiar and tired genre of joke. 'You walk into the [conference room, living room, museum gallery, hospital ward], the contextual intention system recognizes you by your [beacon, tag, badge, face, gait], and the [lights, music, temperature, privacy settings, security permissions] adjust smoothly to your preferences. Your new location is announced to the [room, building, global buddy list service, Homeland Security Department], and your [videoconference, favorite TV show, appointment calendar, breakfast order] is automatically started.' And so on. Of course, what real people need or want in any given situation is *far* from obvious.

It's ironic, then, that one of the things that real people demonstrably do *not* want in their present situation is everyware. There is no constituency for it, no pent-up demand; you'll never hear someone spontaneously express a wish for a ubiquitous house or city. There are days, in fact, when it can seem to me that the entire endeavor has arisen out of some combination of the technically feasible and that which is of interest to people working in human-computer interaction. Or worse, much worse: out of marketing, and the desire to sell people yet more things for which they have neither a legitimate need nor even much in the way of honest desire.

What people do want, and will ask for, is more granular. They want, as Mark Weiser knew so long ago, to be granted a god's-eye view of the available parking spaces nearby, to spend less time fumbling with change at the register, to have fewer different remote controls to figure out and keep track of.

And, of course, everyware is the (or at least *an*) answer to all of these questions. But until those of us in the field are better able to convey this premise to the wider world in convincing and compelling detail, we can expect that adoption will be significantly slower than might otherwise be the case.

Thesis 59

The necessary processor speed already exists.

Of the major limiting factors on ubiquitous computing, one of the most vexing—and certainly the most fundamental—has always been processor speed. The challenges posed by the deployment of computing out in the everyday environment, whether parsing the meaning of a gesture in real time or tracking 500 individual trajectories through an intersection, have always been particularly processor-intensive.

But if processor speed has historically constituted a brake on development, it needn't any longer. The extravagance of computational resources such applications require is now both technically feasible and, at long last, economic.

The machine I am writing these words on operates at a clock speed of 1.5 GHz—that is, the internal clock by which it meters its processes cycles 1.5 billion times every second. While this sounds impressive enough in the abstract, it's not particularly fast, even by contemporary standards. Central processors that operate more than twice as fast are widely commercially available; a 2004 version of Intel's Pentium 4 chip runs at 3.4 GHz, and by the time this book reaches your hands, the CPU inside the most generic of PCs will likely be faster yet.

We know, too, that relying on CPU clock speeds for estimates of maximum speed can be deceptive: such general-purpose chips are held to speeds well below the theoretical maximum, while specialized chips can be optimized to the requirements of a particular application—video or sound processing, encryption, and so on. In synchrony, CPUs and specialized chips already handle with aplomb the elaborate variety of processor-intensive applications familiar from the desktop, from richly immersive games to real-time multiway videoconferencing.

In principle, then, a locally ubiquitous system—say, one dedicated to household management—built right now from commonly available CPUs and supported by a battery of specialized helpers, should be perfectly adequate to the range of routine tasks foreseeable in such a setting. Excepting those problems we've already identified as "AI-hard," which aren't as a rule well-suited to brute-force approaches anyway, there shouldn't be anything in the home beyond the compass of such a system.

Especially if a grid architecture is employed—if, that is, the computational burden imposed by more convoluted processes is distributed through the constellation of locally-embedded processors, working in parallel—today's clock speeds are entirely adequate to deliver services to the user smoothly and reliably. Whatever challenges exist, it's hard to imagine that they would be order-of-magnitude harder than supporting an iRoom-style collaborative workspace, and that was achieved with 2001-vintage processor speeds.

The other side of the speed equation is, of course, expense; one-off showpieces for research labs and corporate "visioning" centers are well and good, but their effects are generally achieved at prohibitive cost. In order to support meaningfully ubiquitous systems, componentry must be cheap. Current projections—and not necessarily the most optimistic—indicate that processors with speeds on the order of 2 GHz will cost about what ordinary household electrical components (e.g., dimmer switches) do now, at the end of the decade or very soon thereafter. This would allow an ordinary-sized room to be provisioned with such an abundance of computational power that it is difficult to imagine it all being used, except as part of some gridlike approach to a particularly intractable problem. Less extravagant implementations could be accomplished at negligible cost.

When there are that many spare processing cycles available, some kind of market mechanism might evolve to allocate them: an invisible agora going on behind the walls, trading in numeric operations. But we can leave such speculations for other times. For the moment, let's simply note that—even should Moore's Law begin to crumble and benchmark speeds stagnate rather than continuing their steep upward climb—processing capacity presents no obstacle to the emergence of full-fledged ubiquitous services.

Thesis 60

The necessary storage capacity already exists.

It's easy to infer that a panoply of ubiquitous systems running at all times—systems whose operation by definition precedes users, as we've noted—is going to churn up enormous quantities of data. How and where is all this information going to be stored? Will the issue of storage itself present any obstacle to the real-world deployment of everyware?

We can derive a useful answer by, again, extrapolating not from the best currently available systems, but from those at the middle of the pack. The iPod shuffle I wear when I go running, for example, is a circa-2004 solid-state storage device, with only incidental moving parts, that boasts a capacity of 1 GB. This is about a day and a half's worth of music encoded with middling fidelity, a few hours' worth at the highest available resolution. It achieves this (as Apple's advertising was pleased to remind us) inside a form factor of around the same volume as a pack of chewing gum, and it's already been rendered obsolete by newer and more capacious models.

A day and a half sure sounds like a decent amount of music to pack into a few cubic centimeters; certainly it's suggestive of what might be achieved if significant parts of a structure were given over to solid-state storage. But hard-ubicomp enthusiasts already dream of far greater things. On a chilly night in Göteborg in late 2002, Lancaster University HCI pioneer Alan Dix described an audacious plan to record in high fidelity every sense impression a human being ever has—favoring me with a very entertaining estimate of the bandwidth of the human sensorium, the total capacity necessary to store all of the experiences of an average lifetime, and a guess as to what volume would suffice to do so: "If we start recording a baby's experiences now, by the time she's 70 all of it will fit into something the size of a grain of sand."

If I recall correctly, Dix's order-of-magnitude guess was that no more than 20 TB (each terabyte is 1,000 GB) would be required to record *every* sensory impression of *any* sort that you have in the entire course of your life. And when you run the numbers—making the critical assumption that increases in storage capacity will continue to slightly outpace the 24-month doubling period specified by Moore's law for transistor density—*mirabile dictu*, it does turn out to be the case that by mid-2033, it will at least theoretically be possible to store that amount of information in a nonvolatile format the size and weight of a current-generation iPod nano. (The grain of sand appears not long thereafter.)

As of the end of 2005, the numbers undernetting this rather science-fictiony-sounding estimate still hold and are maybe even a little conservative. The real point of all this extrapolation, though, is to buy some room for those challenges inherent in everyware that, however daunting they may seem at the moment, are nonetheless of smaller magnitude.

If we can take as a limit case the recording of every single impression experienced in the course of a life, then it seems fair to say that all the other issues we're interested in addressing will be found somewhere inside this envelope. And if this is so—and there's currently little reason to believe otherwise—we can safely assume that even devices with small form factors will be able to contain usefully large storage arrays.

Going a step further still, such high local information densities begin to suggest the Aleph of Borges (and William Gibson): a single, solid-state unit that contains high-fidelity representations of literally everything, "the only place on earth where all places are." As strange as this poetic notion may sound in the context of an engineering discussion, the numbers back it up; it's hard to avoid the conclusion that we are entering a regime in which arbitrarily large bodies of information can be efficiently cached locally, ready to hand for whatever application requires them.

If this is too rich for your blood, Roy Want, Gaetano Boriello, and their co-authors point out, in their 2002 paper "Disappearing Hardware," that we can at least "begin to use storage in extravagant ways, by prefetching, caching and archiving data that might be useful later, lessening the need for continuous network connectivity."

While this is more conservative, and certainly less romantic, than Borges' Aleph, it has the distinct advantage (for our immediate purposes, anyway) of referring to something real. Intel has demonstrated several iterations of a high-density mobile/wearable storage system based on these ideas, called a "personal server," the earliest versions of which were little more than a hard drive with a built-in wireless connection. Where Want's version of Alan Dix's calculation puts that total lifetime throughput figure at a starkly higher 97 TB ("80 years, 16 hours a day, at 512 Kbps"), he reckons that a personal server should store that amount of data by the more optimistic date of 2017; some of the apparent optimism no doubt reflects the difference in scale between a grain of sand and the mobile-phone-sized personal server.

But, again, the purpose of providing such calculations is merely to backstop ourselves. Any ubiquitous application that requires less in the way of local storage than that required by recording every sensation of an entire life in high fidelity would seem to present little problem from here on out.

Thesis 61

The necessary addressing scheme already exists.

As we considered earlier, a technology with the ambition to colonize much of the observable world has to offer some provision for addressing the very large number of nodes implied by such an ambition. We've seen that a provision along these lines appears to exist, in the form of something called IPv6, but what exactly does this cryptic little string mean?

In order to fully understand the implications of IPv6, we have to briefly consider what the Internet was supposed to be "for" in the minds of its original designers, engineers named Robert E. Kahn and Vint Cerf. As it turns out, Kahn and Cerf were unusually prescient, and they did not want to limit their creation to one particular use or set of uses. As a result, from the outset it was designed to be as agnostic as possible regarding the purposes and specifications of the devices connected to it, which has made it a particularly brilliant enabling technology.

The standard undergirding communication over the Internet—a network layer protocol known, rather sensibly, as Internet Protocol, or IP—doesn't stipulate anything but the rules by which packets of ones and zeroes get switched from one location to another. The model assumes that all the intelligence resides in the devices connected to the network, rather than in the network itself. (The term of art engineers use to describe this philosophy of design is "end to end.") As a result, as these things go, the Internet is simple, robust, all but endlessly extensible, and very, very flexible.

For our purposes, the main point of interest of the current-generation IP—version 4—is that it is running out of room. Addresses in IPv4 may be 32 bits long, and the largest number of discrete addresses that it will ever be possible to express in 32 bits turns out to be a little over four billion. This sounds like a comfortably large address space, until you consider that each discrete node of digital functionality ("host") you want to be able to send and receive traffic over the network requires its own address.

The exponential growth of the Internet in all the years since scientists first started sending each other e-mail, and particularly the spike in global traffic following the introduction of the World Wide Web, have swallowed up all of the numeric addresses provided for in the original protocol, many years before its designers thought such a thing possible. It's as if, while building a new settlement in a vast desert, you had somehow begun to run out of street numbers—you can see limitless room for expansion all around you, but it's become practically impossible to build even a single new house because you would no longer be able to distinguish it from all of its neighbors.

This scarcity is one of the stated justifications behind promulgating a new version of IP, version 6. By virtue of extending the length of individual addresses in IPv6 to a generous 128 bits, the address space thus evoked becomes a staggering 2^{128} discrete hosts—roughly equivalent to a number that starts with the numeral 3 and continues for 38 zeroes. That works out to 6.5×10^{23} for every square meter on the surface of the planet. (One commentary on the specification dryly suggests that this "should suffice for the foreseeable future.")

What this means above all is that we no longer need to be parsimonious with IP addresses. They can be broadcast promiscuously, tossed into the world by the bucketload, without diminishing or restricting other possibilities in the slightest. There are quite enough IPv6 addresses that every shoe and stop sign and door and bookshelf and pill in the world can have one of its own, if not several.

The significance of IPv6 to our story is simply that it's a necessary piece of the puzzle—if the role of sufficiently capacious addressing scheme wasn't filled by this particular specification, it would have to be by something else. But everyware needs a framework that provides arbitrarily for the communication of anything with anything else, and IPv6 fills that requirement admirably.

Thesis 62

The necessary display technologies already exist.

Although many—perhaps even the majority of—deployments of everyware will by their nature not require display screens of the conventional sort, there will still be a general requirement for the graphic presentation of information.

With displays of various sorts appearing in an ever greater number of places throughout the environment, though, we can assume that the ethic of calmness we've discussed in other contexts will also inform their design. And this turns out to have a lot to do with screen luminance and resolution, threshold values of which must be reached before the display itself fades from awareness—before, that is, you feel like you're simply working on a document and not on a representation of a document.

With the commercial introduction of Sony's LIBRIé e-book reader in early 2004, display screens would appear to have effectively surmounted the perceptual hurdles associated with such transparency of experience: In reading text on them, you're no more conscious of the fact that you're using a screen than you would ordinarily be aware that you're reading words from a printed page.

The LIBRIé, a collaboration of Sony, Philips Electronics' Emerging Display Technology unit, and startup E Ink, is a relatively low-cost, mass-market product. At 170 pixels per inch, the screen's resolution is not heroically high by contemporary standards—Mac OS defaults to 72 ppi for displaying graphics on monitors, Windows to 96—but text rendered on it "looks like a newspaper" and has left a strongly favorable impression on most of us lucky enough to have seen it.*

The LIBRIé owes much of its *oooooh* factor to E Ink's proprietary microencapsulation technology—a technology which, it must be said, is impressive in many regards. The quality that leaps out at someone encountering it for the first time is its dimensionality. The technique allows conformal screens of so-called "electronic paper" to be printed to the required specifications, and this can result in some striking applications, like the rather futuristic watch prototype the company has produced in collaboration with Seiko, a gently curving arc a few millimeters thick. But it's also versatile—large-scale prototype displays have been produced—and astonishingly vibrant, and it's easy to imagine such units replacing conventional displays in the widest possible variety of applications.**

Nor is E Ink the only party pursuing next-generation displays. Siemens offers a vanishingly thin "electrochromic" display potentially suitable for being printed on cardboard, foil, plastic and paper. These are being envisioned, initially at least, for limited-lifetime applications such as packaging, labels, and tickets; when combined with printable batteries such as those produced by Israeli startup Power Paper, the *Minority*

---

*If Sony had chosen not to cripple the LIBRIé with unreasonably restrictive content and rights-management policies, it's very likely that you, too, would have seen the device. As it is, Sony's regrettable distrust of its own customers has ensured that an otherwise-appealing product ends up atop the dustbin of history.

**None of this is to neglect that other common trope of ubicomp imaginings, the wall- or even building-scale display. A friend once proposed, in this regard, that the Empire State Building be lit each night with a display of color tuned to function as a thermometer—a kind of giant ambient weather beacon.

Report scenario of yammering, full-motion cereal boxes is that much closer to reality.

Commercial products using the E Ink technology, including the Seiko watch, are slated for introduction during 2006; Siemens, meanwhile, plans to introduce 80-dpi electrochromic packaging labels (at a unit cost of around 30 cents) during 2007. The inference we can draw from such developments is that the challenges posed by a general requirement for highly legible ambient display are well on their way to being resolved, at a variety of scales. As a consequence, we can regard the issue of display as posing no further obstacle to the development of ubiquitous systems requiring them.

Thesis 63

**The necessary wireless networking protocols
already exist.**

If IPv6 gives us a way to identify each of the almost unimaginably rich
profusion of nodes everyware will bring into being, we still need to provide some channel by which those nodes can communicate with each
other. We already have some fairly specific ideas of what such a channel should look like: Most of our visions of ubiquity presuppose a network that:

- is wireless;
- provides broadband;
- affords autodiscovery;
- is available wherever you might go.

As it happens, each of them is neatly answered by a brace of emerging
(and in some cases conflicting) networking standards.

At ultra-short range, a new standard called Wireless USB is intended
by its developers to succeed Bluetooth in the personal area networking (PAN) role during 2006-2007, connecting printers, cameras, game
controllers, and other peripherals. Supported by the WiMedia Alliance,
an industry coalition that counts HP, Intel, Microsoft, Nokia, Samsung,
and Sony among its mainstays, Wireless USB is—like similar ultrawide-
band (UWB) protocols—a low-power specification affording connection
speeds of up to 480 Mbps. Undeterred, the industry alliance responsible
for Bluetooth—the Bluetooth Special Interest Group—has announced its
own plans for a new, UWB-compatible generation of their own standard.
(Confusingly enough, the group counts many of the same companies
supporting Wireless USB among its adherents.)

As we've seen, this is sufficient to stream high-definition video between devices in real time. Given that such streams represent something like peak demand on PAN, at least for the foreseeable future, we're probably safe in regarding the challenges of wireless networking at short range as having been overcome upon the introduction of Wireless USB or similar.

Wireless USB and its competing standards, although intended mainly to link peripherals at ranges of a few meters, begin to blur into what has historically been considered the domain of local area networking, or LAN. They certainly offer higher speeds than the current widely-deployed wireless LAN implementation, Wi-Fi: While the 802.11g variant of Wi-Fi provides for a nominal maximum speed of 54 Mbps, in practice, throughput is often limited to a mere fraction of that number and in some cases is barely any faster than the 11 Mbps maximum of the earlier 802.11b standard.

Nor can current-generation Wi-Fi base stations cope with the longer ranges implied by so-called metropolitan area networking, in which regions anywhere up to several kilometers across are suffused with a continuous wash of connectivity. Vulnerable on both the counts of speed and range, then, Wi-Fi will almost certainly be superseded over the next year or two by the new WiMAX standard.

WiMAX isn't some new and improved form of Wi-Fi; it is a relatively radical departure from the Ethernet model from which the 802.11 standard is originally derived. (Some of the blame for this common misperception must clearly be laid at the feet of those who chose to brand the standard thusly.) Fortunately, this does not prevent the standard from offering a certain degree of backward-compatibility with earlier devices, although they will surely not be able to take advantage of all that it has to offer.

And what WiMAX has to offer is impressive: bandwidth sufficient for simultaneous voice over IP, video, and Internet streams, with data rates of 70 Mbps provided over ranges up to a nominal 50 kilometers. The speed is only a little bit faster than the swiftest current flavor of Wi-Fi, 802.11g, but the range is vastly improved. When both WiMAX and Wireless USB have supplanted the current generation of networking standards—as they are supposed to, starting in 2006—we will have three of the four elements we were looking for in our robust ubiquitous network: wireless broadband connectivity, at a range of scales, just about anywhere we might think to go.

This leaves us only the issue of autodiscovery.

One of the less charming provisions of Bluetooth, at least in its earlier incarnations, was that devices equipped with it did not automatically "discover" and recognize one another. They had to be manually paired, which, on the typical mobile phone, meant a tiresome descent through the phone's hierarchy of menus, in search of the one screen where such connectivity options could be toggled.

While establishing a Wi-Fi connection is not typically as onerous as this, it too presents the occasional complication—even Apple's otherwise refined AirPort Extreme implementation of 802.11 confronts the user with a variety of notifications and dialog boxes relating to the current state of connection. When I'm out in the field, for example, my computer still asks me if I'd like to join one or another of the networks it detects, rather than making an educated guess as to the best option and acting on it.

And this is precisely the kind of overinvolvement that a classically Weiserian everyware would do away with; presumably, the task you are actually interested in accomplishing is several levels of abstraction removed from pairing two devices. That is, not only do you not want to be bothered with the granular details of helping devices discover one another, you're not particularly interested in connectivity per se, or even in sending files. These are simply things that must be accomplished before you can engage the task that you originally set out to do.

Autodiscovery, then, however arcane it may sound, is a *sine qua non* of truly ubiquitous connectivity. You shouldn't have to think about it—not if our notions of the encalming periphery are to make any sense at all.*

We should note, however, that this is precisely the kind of situation the doctrine of "beautiful seams" was invented for. If the default setting is for users to be presented with fully automatic network discovery, they should still be offered the choice of a more granular level of control.

But while a smooth treatment of service discovery is indisputably critical to good user experience in ubiquitous computing, it's a question more of individual implementations of a wireless networking technology than of any given protocol itself.

With the near-term appearance of standards such as Wireless USB and WiMAX, the necessary provisions for ubiquitous networking are at last in hand. The question of how to connect devices can itself begin to disappear from consciousness, unless we explicitly desire otherwise.

Thesis 64

The necessary bridges between atoms and bits already exist.

Like a leitmotif, one idea has been woven through this book from its very beginning, popping to the surface in many places and in many ways: The logic of everyware is total. Whether anyone consciously intended it to be this way or not, this is a technology with the potential to sweep every person, object and place in the world into its ambit.

Obviously, though, and for a variety of good reasons, not everything in the world can or should have the necessary instrumentation built into it at design time. Sometimes we'd like to account for something built before everyware was ever contemplated, whether it be a medieval manuscript or a 1970 Citroën DS; sometimes we might want to keep track of something whose nature precludes *ab initio* integration, like a cat, or a can of cranberry sauce, or a stand of bamboo.

So in order for the more total visions of information processing in everyday life to be fully workable, there exists a generic requirement for something that will allow all this otherwise unaugmented stuff of the physical world to exist also in the hyperspace of relational data—a bridge between the realm of atoms and that of bits.

Ideally, such bridges would be reasonably robust, would not require an onboard power supply, and could be applied to the widest possible range of things without harming them. Given the above use scenarios, a very small form factor, a low-visibility profile, or even total imperceptibility would be an advantage. Above all, the proposed bridge should be vanishingly cheap—the better to economically supply all the hundreds of billions of objects in the world with their own identifiers.

Such bridges already exist—and are in fact already widely deployed. We'll limit our discussion here to the two most prominent such technologies: RFID tags and two-dimensional bar-codes.

The acronym RFID simply means "radio-frequency identification," although in use it has come to connote a whole approach to low-cost, low-impact data-collection. There are two fundamental types of RFID tags, "active" and "passive"; just as you'd assume, active tags broadcast while passive tags require scanning before offering up their payload of information.

While both types of tags incorporate a chip and an antenna, passive tags do not require an onboard power supply. This allows them to be extremely cheap, small, and flexible; they can be woven into fabrics, printed onto surfaces, even slapped on in the form of stickers. Of course, this limits their range of action to short distances, no more than a few meters at the very outside, while active RFID units, supplied with their own onboard transmitter and power supply, trade greater range for a correspondingly bulkier profile.

The onboard memory chip generally encodes a unique numeric identifier and includes as well whatever other information is desired about the item of interest: part number, account number, SKU, color.... Really, the possibilities are endless. And it's this flexibility that accounts for the incredibly wide range of RFID applications we see: In everyday life, you're almost certainly already engaging RFID infrastructures, whether you're aware of it or (more likely) not.

Two-dimensional bar codes address some of the same purposes as passive RFID tags, though they require visual scanning (by a laser reader or compatible camera) to return data. While unidimensional bar-codes have seen ubiquitous public use since 1974 as the familiar Universal Product Code, they're sharply limited in terms of information density; newer 2D formats such as Semacode and QR, while perhaps lacking the aesthetic crispness of the classic varieties, allow a literally geometric expansion of the amount of data that can be encoded in a given space.

At present, one of the most interesting uses of 2D codes is when they're used as hyperlinks for the real world. Semacode stickers have been cleverly employed in this role in the Big Games designed by the New York City creative partnership area/code, where they function as markers of buried treasure, in a real-time playfield that encompasses an entire urban area—but what 2D coding looks like in daily practice can perhaps best be seen in Japan, where the QR code has been adopted as a de facto national standard.

QR codes can be found anywhere and everywhere in contemporary Japan: in a product catalogue, in the corner of a magazine ad, on the back of a business card. Snap a picture of one with the camera built into your phone—and almost all Japanese *keitai* are cameraphones—and the phone's browser will take you to the URL it encodes and whatever information waits there. It's simultaneously clumsy and rather clever.

Ultra-low-cost 2D-coded stickers allow what might be called the depositional annotation of the physical world, as demonstrated by the recent Semapedia project. Semapedia connects any given place with a Wikipedia page to that page, by encoding a link to the Wikipedia entry in a sticker. For example, there's a Semapedia sticker slapped up just outside Katz's Delicatessen on the Lower East Side of Manhattan; shoot a picture of the sticker with a compatible cameraphone, and you're taken to the Katz's page on Wikipedia, where you can learn, among other things, precisely how much corned beef the deli serves each week.*

The significance of technologies like RFID and 2D bar-coding is that they offer a low-impact way to "import" physical objects into the datasphere, to endow them with an informational shadow. An avocado, on its own, is just a piece of fleshy green fruit—but an avocado whose skin has been laser-etched with a machine-readable 2D code can tell you how and under what circumstances it was grown, when it was picked, how it was shipped, who sold it to you, and when it'll need to be used by (or thrown out).

Five thousand pounds.

This avocado, that RFID-tagged pallet—each is now relational, searchable, *available* to any suitable purpose or application a robust everyware can devise for it. And of course, if you're interested in literal ubiquity or anything close to it, it surely doesn't hurt that RFID tags and 2D codes are so very cheap.

Richly provisioned with such bridges between the respective worlds of things and of data, there is no reason why everyware cannot already gather the stuff of our lives into the field of its awareness.

Thesis 65

**The necessary standards for the representation
and communication of structured data
already exist.**

From the perspective of someone unfamiliar with the details of contemporary information technology—which is to say most of us—one factor that might seem to stand in the way of everyware's broader diffusion is the wild heterogeneity of the systems involved. We've grown accustomed to the idea that an ATM card issued in Bangor might not always work in Bangkok, that a Bollywood film probably won't play on a DVD player bought in Burbank—so how credible is any conception of the ubiquitous present that relies on the silky-smooth interplay of tag reader and wireless network, database and embedded microcontroller?

However intractable such issues may seem, their solution is in hand— if currently wedged somewhere in the gap between theory and robust praxis. Exactly how is a piece of information represented so that it may be reported by an RFID tag, put into proper perspective by visualization software, correlated with others in a database, and acted on by some remote process? How do such heterogeneous systems ever manage to pass data back and forth as anything more than a stripped-down, decontextualized series of values?

One of the first successful attempts to address such questions was the Standard Generalized Markup Language (SGML), adopted as the international standard ISO 8879 in 1986. SGML was intended to permit the sharing of machine-readable documents between different systems; its fundamental innovation, still observed in all the markup languages descended from it, was to propose that a document be provisioned with interpolated, semantic "tags" describing its various parts.* For example, a document describing this book might mark it up (at least in part) like this:

<title>Everyware</title>

<subtitle>The dawning age of ubiquitous computing</subtitle>

<author>Adam Greenfield</author>

<pubyear>2006</pubyear>

Once a document has been marked up this way, SGML-compliant but otherwise incompatible systems will parse it identically. Moreover, SGML is a metalanguage, a tool kit for the construction of interoperable special-purpose languages; as long as all observe the rules of valid SGML, any number of different applications can be built with it.

This would seem to make SGML the perfect lingua franca for technical systems—in theory, anyway. In practice, the language has some qualities that make it hard to use, most notably its complexity; it was also not ideally suited to the multilingual Internet, where documents might well be rendered in tightly-woven Farsi or the stolid ideograms of Traditional Chinese. In the late 1990s, therefore, a working group of the World Wide Web Consortium developed a streamlined subset of SGML known as XML (for eXtensible Markup Language) specifically designed for use in the Internet context.**

While XML has the very useful quality that it is both machine-readable and (reasonably) legible to people, the source of its present interest to us is the success it has enjoyed in fostering machine-to-machine communication. Since its release in 1998, XML has becoming the lingua franca

---

*Such tags are not to be confused with those of the RFID variety.

**Regrettably, the most recent version of XML still excludes support for several of the world's writing systems, notably the plump curls of Burmese and the hauntingly smokelike vertical drafts of Mongolian Uighur script.

SGML never was, allowing the widest possible array of devices to share data in a manner comprehensible to all.

XML compatibility, inevitably, is not universal, nor has it been perfectly implemented everywhere it has been deployed. But it is a proven, powerful, general solution to the problem of moving structured data across systems of heterogeneous type and capability. Once again, we'll have to look elsewhere if we're interested in understanding why everyware is anything but a matter of the very near term.

Thesis 66

For many of us, everyware is already a reality.

Maybe it's time for a reality check. We should be very clear about the fact that when we raise the question of ubiquitous computing, we're not simply talking about the future—even the near future—but also about things that actually exist now.

Far from presenting itself to us as seamless, though, everyware as it now exists is a messy, hybrid, piecemeal experience, and maybe that's why we don't always recognize it for what it is. It certainly doesn't have the science-fictional sheen of some of the more enthusiastic scenarios.

There are systems in the world that do begin to approach such scenarios in terms of their elegance and imperceptibility. The qualities defined way back in Section 1 as being diagnostic of everyware—information processing embedded in everyday objects, dissolving in behavior—can already be found in systems used by millions of people each day.

We've already discussed PayPass and Blink, the RFID-based payment systems that will receive their large-scale commercial rollouts by the end of 2005. What if they succeed beyond their sponsors' expectations and become a matter-of-fact element of daily life? What if you could use the same system to pay for everything from your mid-morning latte to a few quick copies at the local 7-Eleven to the train home in the evening—all with a jaunty wave of your wrist?

If you've ever visited Hong Kong, or are lucky enough to live there, you know exactly what this would look like: Octopus. Octopus is a contactless, stored-value "smartcard" used for electronic payment throughout Hong Kong, in heavy and increasing daily use since 1997, and it gives us a pretty good idea of what everyware looks like when it's done right.

Appropriately enough, given its origins as a humble transit pass, Octopus can be used on most of the city's wild and heterogeneous tangle of public transportation options, even the famous Star Ferries that ply the harbor.

Even if getting around town were the only thing Octopus could be used for, that would be useful enough. But of course that's *not* all you can do with it, not nearly. The cards are anonymous, as good as cash at an ever-growing number of businesses, from Starbucks to local fashion retailer Bossini. You can use Octopus at vending machines, libraries, parking lots, and public swimming pools. It's quickly replacing keys (card- and otherwise) as the primary means of access to a wide variety of private spaces, from apartment and office buildings to university dorms. Cards can be refilled at just about any convenience store or ATM. And, of course, you can get a mobile with Octopus functionality built right into it, ideal for a place as phone-happy as Hong Kong.*

If this description sounds a little breathless, it's because I have used Octopus myself in many of the above contexts and experienced a little millennial flush of delight every time I did so. The system's slogan is "making everyday life easier," and rarely has a commercial product made so good on its tagline. And if you want to know what "information processing dissolving in behavior" really looks like, catch the way women swing their handbags across the Octopus readers at the turnstiles of the Mong Kok subway station; there's nothing in the slightest to suggest that this casual, 0.3-second gesture is the site of intense technical intervention.

According to the Octopus consortium, 95 percent of Hong Kong citizens between the ages of 16 and 65 use their product; you don't get much more ubiquitous than that. As of late 2004, the last period for which full figures are available, Octopus recorded some eight million transactions a day—more, in other words, than there are people in the city. Is this starting to sound like something real?

Despite the popular "Octo-phone" moniker, Nokia made the canny decision to embed the Octopus RFID unit not in any one model of phone, but in an interchangeable faceplate.

Nor should we make the mistake of thinking that the daily experience of everyware is limited to the other side of the Pacific. Something closer to home for American readers is the E-ZPass electronic toll-collection system, now used on highways, bridges and tunnels throughout the Northeast Corridor.

E-ZPass, like California's FasTrak, is an RFID-based system that lets subscribers sail through toll plazas without stopping: A reader built into the express-lane infrastructure queries dashboard- or windshield-mounted tags and automatically debits the subscriber's account. While the system is limited to highways and parking lots at present, some Long Island McDonald's outlets are experimenting with a pilot program allowing customers to pay for their fries and burgers with debits from their E-ZPass accounts. It's not quite Octopus yet—not by a long shot—but a more useful system is there in embryo, waiting for the confluence of corporate and governmental adoption that would render it truly ubiquitous.*

What fully operational systems such as Octopus and E-ZPass tell us is that privacy concerns, social implications, ethical questions, and practical details of the user experience are no longer matters for conjecture or supposition. With ubiquitous systems finally available for empirical inquiry, these are things we need to focus on today.

---

*In retrospect, the stroke of genius that secured early success for Octopus was enlisting all of Hong Kong's six major transit systems—and thus, indirectly, the majority-partner government itself—in the joint venture. Ordinarily competitors, each had strong incentive to promote the system's wider adoption.

Thesis 67

Everyware is an immediate issue because it will appear to be a commercially reasonable thing to attempt in the near term.

If Octopus isn't a sufficiently robust instance of real-world everyware for you, perhaps you'll be more impressed by what's happening along the Incheon waterfront, some 40 miles southwest of Seoul. Rising from the sea here are 1,500 acres of newly reclaimed land destined to become South Korea's "ubiquitous city," New Songdo.

New Songdo is being designed, literally from the ground up, as a test bed for the fullest possible evocation of ubiquitous technology in everyday life. Like a living catalogue of all the schemes we've spent the last hundred-and-some pages discussing, it will be a place where tossing a used soda can into a recycling bin will result in a credit showing up in your bank account—where a single smartcard will take you from bus to library to bar after work, and straight through your front door. In fact, almost every scenario we've covered is reflected somewhere or another in New Songdo's marketing materials; the developers have even included the pressure-sensitive flooring for the homes of older residents, where it's once again touted as being able to detect falls and summon assistance. It's quite a comprehensive—and audacious—vision.

And while it certainly sounds like something out of AT&T's infamously techno-utopian "You Will" commercials of the early 1990s, New Songdo is entirely real. It's being built right now, at a cost estimated to be somewhere north of $15 billion.

That financing for the project is being provided by international institutions like ABN Amro, as well as Korean heavyweights Kookmin Bank and

Woori Bank, should tell us something. It doesn't even particularly matter whether few of the "enhancements" planned for this or other East Asian "u-cities" pan out entirely as envisioned; it's sufficient that hardheaded, profit-driven businesspeople think there's a reasonable chance of seeing a return on their investment in everyware to lend the notion commercial credibility.

Of course, New Songdo's planners present it to the world as more than just smart floors and RFID-scanning trash cans. It's being promoted as a 21st century trade portal, an English-speaking "Free Economic Zone" richly supplied with multimodal transportation links to the Incheon seaport and the international airport some six miles away. And it's true that banks, even large and savvy ones, have made costly blunders before.

But the fact that such institutions are willing to underwrite a project that places such weight on its ubiquitous underpinnings advances any discussion of the technology to a new and decisive phase. New Songdo isn't about one or two of the prototype systems we've discussed graduating into everyday use; it's something on the order of all of them, all at once, with their performance to spec crucial to the success of a going business concern. This is the most powerful argument yet in favor of rapidly formulating the conventions and standards that might positively affect the way "the u-life" is experienced by the residents of New Songdo and all those who follow.

Thesis 68

Given that, in principle, all of the underpinnings necessary to construct a robust everyware already exist, the time for intervention is now.

The lack of design documentation, the absence of widely agreed-upon standards, the yawning gaps in deployed network infrastructure, and above all the inordinate complexity of many of the challenges involved in everyware certainly suggest that its deployment is in some sense a problem for the longer term. Perhaps we're reading too much into the appearance of a few disarticulated systems; it's possible that the touchless payment systems and tagged cats and self-describing lampposts are not, after all, part of some overarching paradigm.

If, on the other hand, you do see these technologies as implying something altogether larger, then maybe we ought to begin developing a coherent response. It is my sense that if its pieces are all in place—even if only in principle—then the time is apt for us to begin articulating some baseline standards for the ethical and responsible development of user-facing provisions in everyware.

We should do so, in other words, *before* our lives are blanketed with the poorly imagined interfaces, infuriating loops of illogic, and insults to our autonomy that have characterized entirely too much human-machine interaction to date. Especially with genuinely ubiquitous systems like Pay-Pass and Octopus starting to appear, there's a certain urgency to all this.

As it turns out, after some years of seeing his conception of ubicomp garbled—first by "naively optimistic" engineers, and then by "overblown and distorted" depictions of its dangers in the general-interest media—Mark Weiser had given some thought to this. In a 1995 article called "The

Technologist's Responsibilities and Social Change," he enumerated two principles for inventors of "socially dangerous technology":

1. Build it as safe as you can, and build into it all the safeguards to personal values that you can imagine.

2. Tell the world at large that you are doing something dangerous.

In a sense, that's the project of this book, distilled into 32 words.

What Weiser did not speak to on this occasion—and he was heading into the final years of his life, so we will never know just how he would have answered the question—was the issue of timing. *When* is it appropriate to "tell the world at large"? How long should interested parties wait before pointing out that *not* all of the "appropriate safeguards" have been built into the ubiquitous systems we're already being offered?

My guess, in both cases, is that Weiser's response would be the earliest possible moment, when there's still at least the possibility of making a difference. Even if everyware does take the next hundred years to emerge in all its fullness, the time to assert our prerogatives regarding its evolution is now.

Thesis 69

It is ethically incumbent on the designers of ubiquitous systems and environments to afford the human user some protection.

We owe to the poet Delmore Schwartz the observation that "in dreams begin responsibilities." These words were never truer than they are in the context of everyware.

Those of us who have participated in this conversation for the last several years have dreamed a world of limitless interconnection, where any given fact or circumstance can be associated with an immensely large number of others. And despite what we can see of the drawbacks and even dangers implied, we have chosen to build the dream.

If the only people affected by this decision were those making it, that would be one thing. Then it wouldn't really matter what kind of everyware we chose to build for ourselves, any more than I'm affected right now by Steve Mann's cyborg life, or by the existence of someone who's wired every light and speaker in their home to a wood-grained controller they leave on the nightstand. However strange or tacky or pointless such gestures might seem, they harm no one. They're ultimately a matter of individual taste on the part of the person making them and therefore off-limits to regulation in a free society.

But that's not, at all, what is at stake here, is it? By involving other people by the hundreds of millions in our schemes of ubiquity, those of us designing everyware take onto our own shoulders the heaviest possible burden of responsibility for their well-being and safety. We owe it to them to anticipate, wherever possible, the specific circumstances in which our inventions might threaten the free exercise of their interests, and—again, wherever possible—to design such provisions into the things we build that would protect those interests.

This is not paternalism; in fact, it's just the opposite. Where paternalism is the limitation of choice, all I am arguing for is that people be informed just what it is that they are being offered in everyware, at every step of the way, so they can make meaningful decisions about the place they wish it to have in their lives.

The remainder of this book will articulate some general principles we should observe in the development of ubiquitous computing to secure the interests of those people most affected by it.

How might we safeguard our prerogatives in an everyware world?

By now, our picture is essentially complete. We have a reasonably comprehensive understanding of the nature of ubiquitous computing and the forces involved in determining that nature.

How can we, as designers, users, and consumers, ensure that everyware contains provisions preserving our quality of life and safeguarding our fundamental prerogatives?

Thesis 70

It will not be sufficient simply to say, "First, do no harm."

We've agreed that, in order to protect the interests of everyone involved, it would be wise for us to establish some general principles guiding the ethical design and deployment of ubiquitous technology.

The most essential principle is, of course, *first, do no harm*. If everyone contemplating the development of everyware could be relied upon to take this simple idea to heart, thoughtfully and with compassion, there would be very little need to enunciate any of the following.

There are difficulties with such a laissez-faire approach, though. For one thing, it leaves entirely too much unspoken as to what constitutes harm, as to who is at risk, as to what the likely consequences of failure would be. It assumes that everyone developing everyware will do so in complete good faith and will always esteem the abstract-seeming needs of users more highly than market share, the profit motive, or the prerogatives of total information awareness. And, even where developers can be relied upon to act in good faith, it's simply not specific enough to constitute practically useful guidance.

The next best thing, then, is to develop a strategy for ethical development that does take these factors into account—something that spells out the issues in sufficient detail to be of use to developers, that strikes a balance between their needs and those of users, and that incentivizes compliance rather than punish noncompliance.

How might we go about designing such a strategy? Let's consider the fundamental nature of the challenge before us one last time, and with that fresh in mind, articulate a framework that should help us develop wiser, more useful, and more humane instantiations of everyware.

Thesis 71

We're not very good at doing "smart" yet, and we may never be.

After 230 pages in which we've explored the vast and sprawling terrain of everyware in a fair degree of detail, perhaps we would be safe in venturing some guesses about the deeper nature of its challenge.

At root, I see it this way: as a civilization, our production of high-technological artifacts does not yet display anything like the degree of insight, refinement and robustness that toolmakers, furniture artisans, and craftspeople have developed over the thousands of years of their collective endeavor. Our business practices and development methodologies, the complexity of our technology and even the intellectual frameworks we bring to the task, militate against our being able to do so.

Nor have we so far been able to design systems capable of producing inferences about behavior nearly as accurate as those formed in a split-second glance by just about any adult human being.

In other words, we simply don't do "smart" very well yet, and there are good reasons to believe that we may never.

With regard to the tools we build, compare one of the most accomplished fruits of our high technology, Apple's iPod, with just about any piece of furniture—say, an Eames Aluminum Group lounge chair.

The iPod can fail in many more ways than the chair can, yielding to anything from a cracked case to the exhaustion of its battery to a corruption in the software that drives it. By comparison, just about the only way the chair can truly fail is to suffer some catastrophic structural degradation that leaves it unable to support the weight of an occupant.

Nobody needs to be told how to use the lounge chair. "Users" of any age, background, or degree of sophistication can immediately comprehend it, take it in, in almost all of its details, at a single glance. It is self-revealing to the point of transparency. The same can be said of most domestic furniture: you walk on a floor, lie on a bed, put books and DVDs and tchotchkes on shelves, laptops and flowers and dinner on tables. Did anyone ever have to tell you this?

The same cannot be said of the iPod—widely regarded as one of the best thought-out and most elegant digital artifacts ever, demonstrating market-leading insight into users and what they want to do with the things they buy. To someone encountering an iPod for the very first time, it's not obvious what it does or how to get it to do that. It may not even be obvious how to turn the thing on.

You needn't configure the chair, or set its preferences, or worry about compatible file formats. You can take it out of one room or house and drop it into another, and it still works *exactly* the same way as it did before, with no adjustment. It never reminds you that a new version of its firmware is available and that certain of its features will not be available until you do choose to upgrade. As much as I love my iPod, and I do, none of these statements is true of it.

Many particulars of the chair's form and structure result from a long history of incremental improvements, though of course it doesn't hurt that it was designed by a pair of geniuses. It is very well adapted to everyday life, and unless this particular chair affronts your aesthetic sense, it is likely to provide you with all three of the classical Vitruvian virtues of *firmitas, utilitas,* and *venustas:* durability, utility and delight. The iPod, also designed by a genius, is undeniably delightful, but it falls short on the other two scales. Its utility has been compromised to some degree by "feature creep": As a combination music player, address book, calendar, image viewer and video device, it now does more things than its elegantly simple interface can handle gracefully.

But most digital tools people use regularly are not nearly as refined as the iPod. As technology companies go, Apple devotes an exemplary and entirely atypical amount of time, money, and attention to the user experience, and even so, it still gets something wrong from time to time.

Nor, of course, is the issue limited to MP3 players. Digital products and services of all sorts suffer from the same inattention to detail, inability to model user assumptions correctly, and disinclination to perceive interactions from that user's point of view. Even today, you'll occasionally stumble across a high-profile Web site whose navigation seems intentionally designed to perplex and confound. How much worse will it be when the interface we have to puzzle out isn't that of a Web site or an MP3 player, but that of the toilet, the environment-control system, the entire house?

We've come a long, long way from the simple and profound pleasures of relaxing into a chair, wrapping our palms around the warm curve of a mug, or flicking on a lamp when the dusk begins to claim the fading day. If we've, by now, mostly overcome the legendary blinking-12:00 problem that used to afflict so many of us in our dealings with VCRs, that is still emblematic of the kind of thing that happens—and will continue to happen—routinely when complex technology pervades everyday life.

And this only gets more problematic because, as we've seen, so many applications of everyware rely on machine inference, on estimates about higher-level user behavior derived from patterns observed in the flow of data. A perfect example is the "smart coffee cup" Tim Kindberg and Armando Fox refer to in their 2002 article "System Software for Ubiquitous Computing," which "serves as a coffee cup in the usual way, but also contains sensing, processing and networking elements that let it communicate its state (full or empty, held or put down). So, the cup can give colleagues a hint about the state of the cup's owner."

But the word "hint" is well-chosen here, because that's really all the cup will be able to communicate. It may well be that a full mug on my desk implies that I am also in the room, but this is not always going to be the case, and any system that correlates the two facts had better do so pretty loosely. Products and services based on such pattern-recognition already exist in the world—I think of Amazon's "collaborative filtering"–driven recommendation engine—but for the most part, their designers are only now beginning to recognize that they have significantly underestimated the difficulty of deriving meaning from those patterns. The better part of my Amazon recommendations turn out to be utterly worthless—and of all commercial pattern-recognition systems, that's among those with the largest pools of data to draw on.

Lest we forget: "simple" is hard. In fact, Kindberg and Fox remind us that "[s]ome problems routinely put forward [in ubicomp] are actually AI-hard"—that is, as challenging as the creation of an artificial human-level intelligence. The example they offer—whether a technical system can accurately determine whether a meeting is in session in a given conference room, based on the available indicators—could be supplemented with many another. Knowing when a loved one's feelings have been hurt, when a baby is hungry, when confrontation may prove a better strategy than conciliation: These are things that we know in an instant, but that not even the most sensitive pattern-detection engine can determine with any consistency at all.

So there's a certain hubris in daring to intervene, clumsily, in situations that already work reasonably well, and still more in labeling that intervention "smart." If we want to consistently and reliably build ubiquitous systems that do share something of the nature of our finest tools, that do support the finest that is in us, we really will need some help.

Thesis 72

Even acknowledging their contingency, some explicit set of principles would be highly useful to developers and users both.

Almost all of the available literature on ubiquitous computing is academic. That is, it emerges from the methods and viewpoints of applied science as it is practiced in the collective institution of higher education.

As part of their immersion in the scientific method, academics are trained to be descriptive. A proper academic paper in the sciences is neither proscriptive nor prescriptive; it expresses no opinion about what should or should not happen. Much of the discourse around ubiquitous computing has to date been of the descriptive variety: This is a system we contemplate engineering; this is how far we were able to get with it; this is where our assumptions broke down.

But however useful such descriptive methodologies are, they're not particularly well suited to discussions of what ought to be (or ought not to be) built.

This is not to say that such discussions do not take place—of course they do, whether in person over a cold beer, on electronic mailing lists, or in any of the fora where people working in the field gather. The debates I've been lucky enough to witness are learned, wise, contentious, impassioned, occasionally hysterically funny...but they rarely seem to show up in the literature, except as traces. The realism and the critical perspective so often vividly present in these discussions are lost to the record, all but invisible to anyone who only knows ubiquitous computing through conference proceedings and published work.

There have been attempts to return this perspective to written discussions of ubiquitous systems, some more successful than others. Thinkers as varied as the sociologist and anthropologist Anne Galloway, the industrial design provocateurs Dunne & Raby, and symposiarch John Thackara of the Doors of Perception conferences have all considered the question of pervasive computing from a critical perspective. I read Paul Dourish's *Where the Action Is*, particularly, as a passionate call to strip away the layers and layers of abstraction that so often prevent computing from benefiting the people it is intended to serve, people whose choices are both limited and given meaning by their being-in-the-world. But even this most literate of ubicomp writings is not enough—or is, at least, insufficiently explicit to help the working designer.

And that really is the issue: The working designer may not have the inclination, and definitely does not have the time, to trawl Heidegger for insight into the system they are bringing into being. Anybody working under the pressures and constraints of contemporary technology-development practice will need relatively clear-cut principles to abide by and to wield in discussions with the other members of their team.

Moreover, such guidelines would be of clear utility to those procuring and using everyware. If there is a compact, straightforward, and widely agreed-upon set of guidelines, then a given system's compliance with them could be verified and certified for all to see by something analogous to an interoperability mark. We could trust, in encountering such a system, that every practical measure had been taken to secure the maintenance or extension of our prerogatives.

This is just what all of our explorations have been building toward. After considering its definition, its origins, its likely implications, and the timing of its arrival, we are now ready to articulate five principles for the ethical development of everyware, even as we acknowledge that any such set of principles is bound to be contingent, provisional, and incomplete at best.

One final note: While these principles do aim to provide both developers and users with a useful degree of clarity, they do not spell solutions out in detail. Given the early stage of everyware's evolution, and especially everything we've learned about the futility of evaluating a system when it's been decontextualized and stripped of its specific referents to the real world, the principles focus not on how to achieve a given set of ends, but on what ends we should be pursuing in the first place.

Thesis 73

Everyware must default to harmlessness.

The first of our principles concerns what happens when ubiquitous systems fail. What happens when a critical percentage of sensors short out, when the building's active lateral bracing breaks down, when weather conditions disrupt the tenuous wireless connection? Or what if there's a blackout?

"Graceful degradation" is a term used in engineering to express the ideal that if a system fails, if at all possible it should fail gently in preference to catastrophically; functionality should be lost progressively, not all at once. A Web browser might be unable to apply the proper style sheet to a site's text, but it will still serve you with the unstyled text, instead of leaving you gazing at a blank screen; if your car's ABS module goes out, you lose its assistance in autopumping the brakes ten times a second, but you can still press down on the brake pedal in order to slow the car.

Graceful degradation is nice, but it doesn't go nearly far enough for our purposes. Given the assumption of responsibility inherent in everyware, we must go a good deal further. *Ubiquitous systems must default to a mode that ensures users' physical, psychic, and financial safety.*

Note that this is not an injunction to keep subjects safe at all times: That is as ridiculous as it would be undesirable. It's simply, rather, a strong suggestion that when everyware breaks down—as it surely will from time to time, just like every other technical system that humanity has ever imagined—it should do so in a way that safeguards the people relying on it.

What precisely "safety" means will obviously vary with place and time. Even as regards physical safety alone, in the United States, we find ourselves in a highly risk-averse era, in which public fear and litigiousness place real limits on what can be proposed. (A playground surface that no German would think twice about letting their children frolic on simply wouldn't fly in the States, and I sometimes wonder what our media would do to fill airtime were it not for flesh-eating bacteria, bloodthirsty sharks, missing blonde women, and al-Qaida sleeper cells.)

Coming to agreement as to what constitutes psychic and financial safety is probably more culture-dependent still. So it's entirely possible that working out a definition of safety broad enough to be shared will leave few parties wholly content.

But the ubiquitous systems we're talking about engage the most sensitive things in our lives—our bodies, our bank accounts, our very identities—and we should demand that a commensurately high level of protection be afforded these things.

Thesis 74

Everyware must be self-disclosing.

The second principle of ethical development concerns provisions to notify us when we are in the presence of some informatic system, however intangible or imperceptible it otherwise may be.

We've seen that everyware is hard to see for a variety of reasons, some circumstantial and some intentional. Information processing can be embedded in mundane objects, secreted away in architectural surfaces, even diffused into behavior. And as much as this may serve to encalm, it also lends itself to too many scenarios in which personal information, including that of the most intimate sort, can be collected without your awareness, let alone your consent.

Given the degree to which ubiquitous systems will be interconnected, information once collected can easily, even inadvertently, be conveyed to parties unknown, operating outside the immediate context.

This is an unacceptable infringement on your right of self-determination. Simply put, you should know what kinds of information-gathering activities are transpiring in a given place, what specific types of information are being collected, and by whom and for what purpose. Finally, you should be told how and in what ways the information-gathering system at hand is connected to others, even if just as a general notification that the system is part of the global net.

We might express such an imperative like this: *Ubiquitous systems must contain provisions for immediate and transparent querying of their ownership, use, and capabilities.*

Everyware must, in other words, be self-disclosing. Such disclosures ensure that you are empowered to make informed decisions as to the level of exposure you wish to entertain.

So, for example, if the flooring in eldercare housing is designed to register impacts, it should say so, as well as specifying the threshold of force necessary to trigger an alert. If the flooring does register a fall, what is supposed to happen? If the flooring is connected in some way to a local hospital or ambulance dispatcher, *which* hospital is it? Even in such an apparently benign implementation of everyware—and maybe even especially in such cases—the choices made by designers should always be available for inspection, if not modification.

None of this is to say that users should be confronted with a mire of useless detail. But seamlessness must be an optional mode of presentation, not a mandatory or inescapable one.

Less ominously, though, such disclosures also help us know when otherwise intangible services are available to us. When an otherwise unremarkable object affords some surprising functionality, or when a digital overlay of information about some place exists, we need to have some way of knowing these things that does not itself rely on digital mediation.

Design researcher Timo Arnall has developed a vocabulary of graphic icons that communicate ideas like these: a friendly, human-readable equivalent of the "service discovery layer" in Bluetooth that specifies what devices and services are locally available. Perhaps Arnall's icons could serve as the basis of a more general graphic language for ubiquitous systems—a set of signs that would eventually become as familiar as "information" or "bathroom," conveying vital ideas of the everyware age: "This object has invisible qualities," or "network dead zone."

Whether we use them to protect ourselves from intrusive information collection or to discover all the ways our new technology can be used, provisions for transparent self-disclosure on the part of ubiquitous systems will be of critical importance in helping us find ways to live around and with them. Such knowledge is the basis of any meaningful ability on our part to decide when and to what degree we wish to engage with everyware and when we would prefer not to.

Thesis 75

Everyware must be conservative of face.

Something too rarely considered by the designers of ubiquitous systems is how easily their ordinary operation can place a user's reputation and sense of dignity and worth at risk.

Thomas Disch illustrates this beautifully in his classic 1973 novel *334*. The grimly futuristic Manhattan of *334* is a place whose entropic spiral is punctuated only by the transient joys of pills, commercial jingles, and empty sex. The world-weary residents of 334 East 13th Street survive under the aegis of a government welfare agency called MODICUM, a kind of Great Society program gone terminally sour.

In particular, *334*'s casual sketch of what would later be known as an Active Badge system hews close to this less-than-heroic theme. Disch shows us not the convenience of such a system, but how it might humiliate its human clients—in this case the aging, preoccupied hospital attendant Arnold Chapel. Embroiled in an illicit plot, Chapel has allowed himself to wander from his course, and is audibly corrected by the hospital's ubiquitous traffic control system:

> "Arnold Chapel," a voice over the PA said. "Please return along 'K' corridor to 'K' elevator bank. Arnold Chapel, please return along 'K' corridor to 'K' elevator bank."

> Obediently he reversed the cart and returned to 'K' elevator bank. His identification badge had cued the traffic control system. It had been years since the computer had had to correct him out loud.

All that was, in fact, necessary or desirable in this scenario was that the system return Chapel to his proper route. Is there any justification, therefore, for the broadcast of information embarrassing to him? Why humiliate, when adjustment is all that is mandated?

Of course, no system in the world can keep people from making fools of themselves. About all that we can properly ask for is that our technology be designed in such a way that it is *conservative of face*: that *ubiquitous systems must not act in such a manner as would unduly embarrass or humiliate users, or expose them to ridicule or social opprobrium, in the course of normal operations.*

The ramifications of such an imperative in a fully-developed everyware are surprisingly broad. With so many systems potentially able to provide the location of users in space and time, we've seen that finding people will become trivially easy. We also know that when facts about your location are gathered alongside other facts—who you are with, what time it is, what sorts of services happen to be available nearby—and subjected to data-mining operations, a relational system can begin to paint a picture of your behavior.

Whether this should be an accurate picture or not—and remember everything we said about the accuracy of machine inference—the revelation of such information can lead to awkward questions about our activities and intentions, the kind we'd rather not have to answer. Even if we didn't happen to be doing anything "wrong," we will still naturally resent the idea that we should answer to anyone else for our choices.

Our concern here goes beyond information privacy per se, to the instinctual recognition that no human community can survive the total evaporation of its membrane of protective hypocrisy. We lie to each other all the time, we dissemble and hedge, and these face-saving mechanisms are critical to the coherence of our society.

So some degree of plausible deniability, including, above all, imprecision of location, is probably necessary to the psychic health of a given community, such that even (natural or machine-assisted) inferences about intention and conduct may be forestalled at will.

How might we be afforded such plausible deniability? In a paper on seamfulness, Ian MacColl, Matthew Chalmers, and their co-authors give us a hint. They describe an ultrasonic location system as "subject to error, leading to uncertainty about...position," and, as they recognized, this imprecision can within reasonable limits be a good thing. It can serve our ends, by giving anyone looking for you most of the information they need about where you are, but not a pinpoint granular location that might lend itself to unwelcome inference.

The degree to which location becomes problematic depends to some extent on which of two alternative strategies is adopted in presenting it. In a "pessimistic" presentation, only verifiably and redundantly known information is displayed, while an "optimistic" display includes possibles, values with a weaker claim on truth. The less parsimonious optimistic strategy obviously presents the specter of false positives, but if this is less than desirable in ordinary circumstances, in this context, a cloud of possible locations bracketing the true one might be just the thing we want. Still worse than the prospect of being nakedly accountable to an unseen, omnipresent network is being nakedly accountable to each other, at all times and places.

Some critics have insisted that there are, at least occasionally, legitimate social purposes invoked in using technology to shame. They point to the example of Korea's notorious "Dogshit Girl," a self-absorbed young lady whose fashion-accessory pet soiled a subway car; having made not the slightest effort to clean it up, she was immediately moblogged by angry onlookers. The pictures appeared online within minutes and throughout the national press after a few hours; according to the Korean press, her humiliation was so total that the young lady eventually withdrew from university.

The argument is that, had the technology not been in place to record her face and present it for all the world to see (and judge), she would have escaped accountability for her actions. There would have been no national furor to serve—ostensibly, anyway—as deterrent against future transgressions along the same lines.

As to whether hounding someone until she feels compelled to quit school and become a recluse can really be considered "accountability" for such a relatively minor infraction, well, thereof we must be silent. Whatever the merits of this particular case, though, there is no doubt that shame is occasionally as important to the coherence of a community as hypocrisy is in another context.

But we are not talking about doing away with shame. The issue at hand is preventing ubiquitous systems from presenting our actions to one another in too perfect a fidelity—in too high a resolution, as it were—and therefore keeping us from maintaining the beneficial illusions that allow us to live as a community. Where everyware contains the inherent potential to multiply the various border crossings that do so much to damage our trust and regard for one other, we must design it instead so that it affords us moments of amnesty. We must build ourselves safe harbors in which to hide from the organs of an accountability that otherwise tends toward the total.

Finally, as we've seen, there is the humiliation and damage to self-worth we experience when we simply can't figure out how to use a poorly designed technical system of any sort. Sadly, no principle or guideline—however strongly stated, however widely observed—can ever endow all the world's designers with equal measures of skill, diligence, and compassion. Nor could any guideline ensure that designers are afforded the time and space they require to work out the details of humane systems. What we can insist on, however, is that those tasked with the development of everyware be reminded of the degree to which our sense of ourselves rides on the choices they make.

Thesis 76

Everyware must be conservative of time.

One of the reasons that the Fukasawan vision of information processing dissolving in behavior is so alluring is because it promises to restore a little simplicity to our world. As a recent ethnographic study by Scott Mainwaring, Ken Anderson, and Michele Chang of Intel Research underscores, daily life in the developed world now exposes us to a multitude of physical and informational infrastructures, each of which requires some kind of token to mediate. Simply to get through the day, we carry keys, cash, credit cards, debit cards, transit passes, parking receipts, library cards, loyalty-program cards—and this list is anything but comprehensive.

Moreover, in the course of a single day we may use any or all of an extensive inventory of digital tools and devices, each of which has a different user interface, each of which behaves differently: music and video players, telephones, personal computers, cameras, cable and satellite television controllers, ATMs, household appliances, even vehicles.

Everyware, of course, promises to replace this unseemly shambles with a compact and intuitive complement of interface provisions, ones that require far less of our time, energy and attention to deal with. The appeal of this paradoxical vision—it might be called high complexity in the service of simplicity—should not be underestimated. But the inevitable flipside of it, at least if our experience with other information technologies is an accurate guide, is that almost all users will face the prospect of wasted time and effort at one time or another.

Philip K. Dick, never one to overlook the all-too-human complications likely in any encounter with high technology, depicted more than one hapless protagonist wrestling with ornery or outright recalcitrant pervasive devices.

In (appropriately enough) *Ubik,* Joe Chip is threatened with a lawsuit by his front door:

> The door refused to open. It said, "Five cents, please."
>
> He searched his pockets. No more coins; nothing. "I'll pay you tomorrow," he told the door. Again he tried the knob. Again it remained locked tight. "What I pay you," he informed it, "is in the nature of a gratuity; I don't have to pay you."
>
> "I think otherwise," the door said. "Look in the purchase contract you signed when you bought this [apartment]."
>
> In his desk drawer he found the contract...Sure enough; payment to his door for opening and shutting constituted a mandatory fee. Not a tip.
>
> "You discover I'm right," the door said. It sounded smug.
>
> From the drawer beside the sink Joe Chip got a stainless steel knife; with it he began systematically to unscrew the bolt assembly of his apt's money-gulping door.
>
> "I'll sue you," the door said as the first screw fell out.
>
> Joe Chip said, "I've never been sued by a door before. But I guess I can live through it."

And this is just to get out of the house and on with his day. Self-important doors are probably not even the worst of it, either; this is the kind of moment we can see strewn through our days, like landmines in the meadows, upon the introduction of an incompetent ubiquitous technology. Accordingly, we should assert as a principle the idea that *ubiquitous systems must not introduce undue complications into ordinary operations.*

You should be able to open a window, place a book upon a shelf, or boil a kettle of water without being asked if you "really" want to do so, or having fine-grained control of the situation wrested away from you. You should not have to configure, manage, or monitor the behavior of a ubiquitous system intervening in these or similar situations—not, at least, after the first time you use it or bring it into some new context. Furthermore, in the absence of other information, the system's default assumption must be that you, as a competent adult, know and understand what you want to achieve and have accurately expressed that desire in your commands.

By the same token, wherever possible, a universal undo convention similar to the keyboard sequence "Ctrl-Z" should be afforded; "save states" or the equivalent must be rolling, continuous, and persistently accessible in a graceful and reasonably intuitive manner. If you want to undo a mistake, or return to an earlier stage in an articulated process, you should be able to specify how many steps or minutes' progress you'd like to efface.

You shouldn't have to work three or four times as hard to achieve some utterly mundane effect (like drawing a bath, starting a car or sharing contact information with a new acquaintance) with everyware as you would have without its putative assistance. Nor should you be forced to spend more time fixing the mess resulting from some momentary slip in a sequence of interactions than the entire process should have taken in the first place.

Will this occasionally approach "AI-hard?" Probably. Nevertheless, we should insist on excluding ubiquitous systems from our everyday lives unless they are demonstrably more respectful of our time than information technologies have tended to be in the past.

Thesis 77

Everyware must be deniable.

Our last principle is perhaps the hardest to observe: *Ubiquitous systems must offer users the ability to opt out, always and at any point.*

You should have the ability to simply say "no," in other words. You should be able to shut down the ubiquitous systems you own and face no penalty other than being unable to take advantage of whatever benefits they offered in the first place. This means, of course, that realistic alternatives must exist.

If you still want to use an "old-fashioned" key to get into your house, and not have to have an RFID tag subcutaneously implanted in the fleshy part of your hand, well, you should be able to do that. If you want to pay cash for your purchases rather than tapping and going, you should be able to do that too. And if you want to stop your networked bathtub or running shoe or car in the middle of executing some sequence, so that you can take over control, there should be nothing to stand in your way.

In fact—and here is the deepest of all of the challenges these principles impose on developers and on societies—where the private sphere is concerned, you should be able to go about all the business of an adult life without ever once being compelled to engage the tendrils of some ubiquitous informatic system.

In public, where matters are obviously more complicated, you must at least be afforded the opportunity to avoid such tendrils. The mode of circumvention you're offered doesn't necessarily have to be pretty, but you should always be able to opt out, do so without incurring undue inconvenience, and above all without bringing suspicion onto yourself. At the absolute minimum, ubiquitous systems with surveillant capacity must announce themselves as such, from safely beyond their fields of operation, in such a way that you can effectively evade them.

The measure used to alert you needn't be anything more elaborate than the signs we already see in ATM lobbies, or anywhere else surveillance cameras are deployed, warning us that our image is about to be captured—but such measures must exist.

Better still is when the measures allowing us to choose alternative courses of action are themselves networked, persistently and remotely available. Media Lab researcher Tad Hirsch's Critical Cartography project is an excellent prototype of the kind of thing that will be required: it's a Web-based map of surveillance cameras in Manhattan, allowing those of us who would rather not be caught on video to plan journeys through the city that avoid the cameras' field of vision. (Hirsch's project also observes a few important provisions of our principle of self-disclosure: His application includes information about where cameras are pointed and who owns them.)

All of the wonderful things our ubiquitous technology will do for us—and here I'm not being sarcastic; I believe that some significant benefits await our adoption of this technology—will mean little if we don't, as individuals, have genuine power to evaluate its merits on our own terms and make decisions accordingly. We must see that everyware serves us, and when it does not, we must be afforded the ability to shut it down. Even in the unlikely event that every detail of its implementation is handled perfectly and in a manner consistent with our highest ambitions, a paradise without choice is no paradise at all.

Thesis 78

Measures aimed at securing our prerogatives via technical means will also appear.

It's not as if the people now developing ubiquitous systems are blind to the more problematic implications of their work—not all of them, anyway, and not by a long stretch. But perhaps unsurprisingly, when they think of means to address these implications, they tend to consider technical solutions first.

Consider the ethic that your image belongs to you—that in private space, anyway, you have the right to determine who is allowed to record that image and what is done with it. At the seventh annual Ubicomp conference, held in Tokyo in September 2005, a team from the Georgia Institute of Technology demonstrated an ingenious system that would uphold this ethic by defeating unwanted digital photography, whether overt or surreptitious.

By relying on the distinctive optical signature of the charge-coupled devices (CCDs) digital cameras are built around, the Georgia Tech system acquires any camera aimed its way in fractions of a second, and dazzles it with a precisely-calibrated flare of light. Such images as the camera manages to capture are blown out, utterly illegible. As demonstrated in Tokyo, it was both effective and inspiring.

Georgia Tech's demo seemed at first blush to be oriented less toward the individual's right to privacy than toward the needs of institutions attempting to secure themselves against digital observation—whether it might be Honda wanting to make sure that snaps of next year's Civic don't prematurely leak to the enthusiast press, or the Transportation Security Agency trying to thwart the casing of their arrangements at

LAX. But it was nevertheless fairly evident that, should the system prove effective under real-world conditions, there was nothing in principle that would keep some equivalent from being deployed on a personal level.

This functions as a timely reminder that there are other ways to protect ourselves and our prerogatives from the less salutary impacts of ubiquitous technology than the guidelines contemplated here. There will always be technical means: various tools, hacks and fixes intended to secure our rights for us, from Dunne & Raby's protective art objects to the (notional) RFIDwasher, a keyfob-sized device that enables its users "to locate RFID tags and destroy them forever!" Some will argue that such material strategies are more efficient, more practical, or more likely to succeed than any assertion of professional ethics.

Thesis 79

Technical measures intended to secure our prerogatives may ignite an arms race or otherwise muddy the issue.

However clever the Georgia Tech system was as a proof of concept—and it made for an impressive demo—there were factors it was not able to account for. For example, it could not prevent photographers using digital SLR cameras (or, indeed, conventional, film-based cameras of any kind) from acquiring images. This was immediately pointed out by optics-savvy members of the audience and openly acknowledged by the designers.

If you were among those in the audience that day in Tokyo, you might have noticed that the discussion took a 90-degree turn at that point. It became one of measures and countermeasures, gambits and responses, ways to game the system and ways to bolster its effectiveness. Thirty seconds after the last echo of applause had faded from the room, we were already into the opening moments of a classic arms race.

This may well be how evolution works, but it has the unfortunate effect of accommodating instead of challenging the idea that, for example, someone has the right to take your image, on your property, without your knowledge or consent. It's a reframing of the discussion on ground that is potentially inimical to our concerns.

Admittedly, this was a presentation of a prototype system at an academic technology conference, not an Oxford Union debate on the ethics of image and representation in late capitalism. But isn't that just the point? Once we've made the decision to rely on an ecology of tools for our protection—tools made on our behalf, by those with the necessary technical expertise—we've let the chance to assert our own prerogatives slip away. *An* ethics will inevitably be inscribed in the design of such tools, but it needn't be ours or anything we'd even remotely consider endorsing. And once the initiative slips from our grasp, it's not likely to be returned to us for a very long time.

We know, too, that such coevolutionary spirals tend to stretch on without end. There's rarely, if ever, a permanent technical solution in cases like this: There are always bigger guns and thicker grades of armor, more insidious viruses and more effective security patches.

From my point of view, then, technical solutions to ethical challenges are themselves problematic. I'm not suggesting that we do without them entirely. I'm saying, rather, that technical measures and ethical guidelines ought to be seen as complementary strategies, most effective when brought to bear on the problem of everyware together. And that where we do adopt technical means to address the social, political, and psychological challenges of ubiquitous technology, that adoption must be understood by all to be without prejudice to the exercise of our ethical prerogatives.

Thesis 80

**The principles we've enunciated can be
meaningfully asserted through voluntary
compliance.**

One of the obvious difficulties with any set of principles such as the ones
we've been discussing concerns the matter of compliance—or, looked at
another way, enforcement.

Can developers working on everyware reasonably be expected to police
themselves, to spend the extra time and effort necessary to ensure that
the systems they produce do not harm or unduly embarrass us, waste
our time, or otherwise infringe on our prerogatives?

Will such guidelines simply be bypassed, going unobserved for the usual
gamut of reasons, from ignorance to incompetence to unscrupulous-
ness? Or will any such self-policing approach be rendered irrelevant by
governmental attempts to regulate everyware?

No response to the drawbacks of everyware will be anything close to perfect. Even if we could assume that all of the practical challenges posed
by our embrace of ubiquitous systems were tractable, there will always
be bad actors of one sort or another.

Given the almost unlimited potential of everyware to facilitate the collection of all sorts of information, the extreme subtlety with which ubiquitous
systems can be deployed, and the notable propensity of certain parties—corporate, governmental—to indulge in overreaching information-
gathering activities if once granted the technical wherewithal, I would be
very surprised if we didn't see some highly abusive uses of this technology over the next few years. I don't think they can be stopped, any more
than spammers, script kiddies, and Nigerian scam artists can be.

Without dismissing these perils in any way, I am actually less worried about them than about the degraded quality of life we are sure to experience if poorly designed everyware is foisted upon us. I believe that this latter set of challenges *can* be meaningfully addressed by collective, voluntary means, like the five principles offered in this book. If standards for the ethical and responsible development of everyware can be agreed upon by a visible cohort of developers, the onus will be on others to comply with them. Given an articulate and persuasive enough presentation of the reasoning behind the principles, those of us committed to upholding them might even find the momentum on our side.

If you think this scenario sounds unduly optimistic, recent technological history offers some support for it. Starting in 1998, a grassroots movement of independent developers demanding so-called "Web standards" forced the hand of industry giants like Microsoft and Netscape, and in not such a terribly long period of time, either.

Within a few years, any major browser you cared to download was compliant with the set of standards the activists had pushed for. The combination of structural and presentational techniques the so-called "standardistas" insisted on is now considered a benchmark of responsible Web development. By any measure, this is a very successful example of bottom-up pressure resulting in wholesale improvements to the shared technological environment.

The standardistas, it must be said, were on the right side of an emerging business calculus to begin with: by the time the movement came to prominence, it was already punitively expensive for developers to code six or seven different versions of a site simply to render properly in all the incompatible browsers then popular. They also enjoyed the advantage of urging their changes on a relatively concentrated decision nexus, at least where the browser-makers were concerned.

And before we get too enthusiastic about this precedent, and what it may or may not imply for us, we should remind ourselves that ensuring that a given ubiquitous system respects our prerogatives will be many orders of magnitude more difficult than ascertaining a Web site's compliance with the relevant standards. The latter, after all, can be verified by running a site's source code through an automated validator. By contrast, we've seen how much room for interpretation there is in defining "undue complications," let alone in determining what might constitute "harm" or "embarrassment." The grey areas are legion compared to the simple, binary truths of Web standards: Either a site is coded in well-formed XHTML, or it is not.

Nevertheless, at its core, the story of Web standards is both inspiring and relevant to our concerns: the coordinated action of independent professionals and highly motivated, self-educated amateurs did change the course of an industry not particularly known for its flexibility. As a direct result, the browsers that the overwhelming majority of us use today are more powerful, the experience of using compliant Web sites is vastly improved, and untold economies have been realized by the developers of both. Rarely has any circumstance in information technology been quite so "win/win/win."

We've seen the various complications that attend technical solutions to the problems of everyware. And we also have abundant reason to believe that governmental regulation of development, by itself, is unlikely to produce the most desirable outcomes. But in the saga of Web standards, we have an object lesson in the power of bottom-up self-regulation to achieve ends in technological development that are both complex and broadly beneficial.

So I see a real hope in the idea that a constituency of enlightened developers and empowered users will attend the rise of everyware, demanding responsible and compassionate design of ubiquitous technology. I further hope that the principles I've offered here are a meaningful contribution to the discussion, that they shed some light on what responsible and compassionate everyware might look like.

I have one final thought on the question of principles and self-guided development. It's clear that an approach such as the one I've outlined here will require articulate, knowledgeable, energetic, and above all visible advocacy if it has any chance of success. But it requires something else, as well: a simple, clear way for users and consumers to know when a system whose adoption they are contemplating complies with the standards they wish to support.

What I would like to see is something along the lines of the Snell certification for auto-racing and motorcycle helmets—or better yet, the projected ISO standards for environmental safety in nanotechnological engineering. This would be a finding of fitness verified by an independent, transparent, and international licensing body: a guarantee to all concerned that to the degree possible, the ubiquitous system in question had been found to observe all necessary protections of the human user. (Such certifications, of course, would do little to protect us from harmful emergent behavior of interacting systems, but neither would they be without value.)

A mechanism such as this means that we can feel safer in harnessing the power of the market to regulate the development of everyware, *because the market will have been provided with accurate and appropriate information.* A simple, high-visibility marker lets people make informed decisions: Either this system meets the guidelines as they existed at such-and-such a date, or it does not. The guidelines are of course there to peruse in detail should anyone wish to do so, but it's not necessary to have a comprehensive understanding of what they mean at the time of purchase, download, or installation. Everything a user needs to know is right there in the certification.

If sentiment in support of these ideas attains critical mass, we reach a point past which buy-in becomes lock-in. From that point forward, most of the everyware we encounter will have been designed and engineered with a deep consideration for our needs and prerogatives.

The aim, of course, is to build a world in which we get to enjoy as many of the benefits of everyware as possible while incurring the smallest achievable cost. I think this is doable, but to a greater extent than has usually been the case, it's not going to come easily. If we want all of these things, we'll have to:

- educate ourselves as to the nature of the various technologies I have here grouped under the rubric of everyware;
- decide which of them we will invite into our lives, and under what circumstances;
- demand that the technologies we are offered respect our claims to privacy, self-determination, and the quality of life;
- and (hardest of all) consistently act in accordance with our beliefs—at work, at the cash register, and at the polls.

Everyware promises so much more than simply smoothing the hassles we experience in our interactions with computers. It aims to rebuild the relationship between computer and user from the ground up, extend the power of computational awareness to every corner of our lives, and offer us vastly more timely, accurate, and useful knowledge of our surroundings, our communities, and ourselves in so doing. It is, in fact, the best candidate yet to become that "sufficiently advanced" technology Arthur C. Clarke so famously described as being "indistinguishable from magic."

We can have it, if we want it badly enough. But the hour is later than we know, the challenges are many and daunting, and most of us barely have an inkling that there's anything to be concerned about in the advent of the next computing. We have our work cut out for us.

Thesis 81

**These principles are necessary but not sufficient:
they constitute not an end, but a beginning.**

Conclusion

ALWAYS CRASHING IN THE SAME CAR

Each morning, upon waking, I indulge myself in the austerities of Buddhist meditation—Korean Zen Buddhism, to be precise, of the Kwan Um School. I sit, empty my mind to the extent that I am able to, and...breathe.

I've been doing this every day for more than 10 years now, absolutely without fail. I've meditated in apartments, barracks, mountain temples, hotel rooms beyond number, on more than one 747 deep in the trans-Pacific night, and once, particularly memorably, in the canvas-webbed cargo bay of a Chinook helicopter chittering its way into a landing zone. It's become one of the few constants of a willfully nomadic and fluid life.

And it's one of the many things in my life that I cannot conceive of being improved by an overlay of ubiquitous information technology. Going for a long run in a warm gentle rain, gratefully and carefully easing my body into the swelter of a hot springs, listening to the first snowfall of winter, savoring the texture of my wife's lips...these are all things that acquire little or no added value by virtue of being networked, relational, correlated to my other activities. They're already perfect, just as they stand.

Even where the application of ubiquitous technology would clearly be useful, I know enough about how informatic systems are built and brought to market to be very skeptical about its chances of bringing wholesale improvement to the quality of my life.

Sure, I'd love to know when my friend Jamie is within a few blocks of my present location and available for a few pints of Guinness. I'd surely appreciate a little help finding the variety of tools and important documents I've stashed somewhere around the house and immediately forgotten. And I would not at all mind if my daily excursions and transactions were eased by the near-universal adoption of something along the lines of Hong Kong's Octopus system.

But I have a hard time buying into the notion that such ubiquitous interventions in the world can be had without significant cost. I see how readily the infrastructure that gets us these amenities also lends itself to repression, exclusion and the reinscription of class and other sorts of privilege. Above all, I see it occasioning hassle...unending hassle. I can't see that we'll derive much net improvement in quality of life from these and the other things everyware promises us—not unless we are exceedingly careful in devising and implementing the technology that undergirds them.

Nor do I see any reason to follow Teruyasu Murakami of Nomura Research in asking how the users of ubiquitous systems can "change their basic value systems to adapt to the new situation." Not only do I think this is a very, very bad idea, but it's also likely to be a painfully drawn-out exercise in futility.

We are who we are, in other words, in all the infuriating and delightful lineaments of our humanity. No matter how "convenient" it would be for us to learn to think and act in ways that accord with the technology we use, I very much doubt whether such a thing is practically achievable. Besides, we've seen what happens when we attempt to forge a New Man: the results are not pretty, to very large values of "not."

So maybe it would be wiser to develop an everyware that suits us, as opposed to the other way around—not that this will be very much easier. In fact, if you get nothing else from this book, I hope you at least come away from it with an understanding of how richly nuanced everyday life turns out to be and how difficult it will be to design ubiquitous systems sophisticated enough to capture those nuances.

We seem to have a hard time with the notion that some aspects of life are simply too important, too meaningful, and too delicate to subject to the rather clumsy interventions of our present information technology. Moreover, anyone venturing to question the wisdom of such interventions risks being branded a neo-Luddite, or worse. In his 1999 *e-topia*, MIT Media Lab professor William Mitchell rather blithely mocked "dogmatic and deterministic Chicken Little" perspectives on technology, dismissing out of hand "those now-familiar glum assertions that the digital revolution must inevitably reinscribe the nastier existing patterns of power and privilege, while trampling on treasured traditions as it does so."

Frankly, I find Mitchell's disdainful tone unjustified, even bizarre. While I don't believe anything in the world is engraved in stone, I do think that each technology we invent contains certain inherent potentials for use. I also think we're foolish if we do not at least consider these potentials and where they lead to undesirable outcomes, take pains to circumvent them.

What seems lost on Mitchell, and on the many others holding similar views, is that the point of raising such questions—at least as far as I am concerned—is not to scuttle ubiquitous technology, but to improve it.

It is axiomatic in the field of biofeedback that "control follows awareness"—you cannot seek to steer some process, that is, until you become conscious of it. My hope in writing this book is to foster a wider awareness of the deep issues raised by everyware, so we can together make the decisions about its emergence that we so urgently need to. And my fundamental point is that the outcome does not have to be something that simply happens to us. To the degree that we, the users and consumers of ubiquitous computing, educate ourselves and take action correspondingly, we get to choose the outcome.

When the stakes are as high as they are here, we must interrogate without mercy the value propositions we're presented and adopt only those ubiquitous products and services that really do improve our lives. In life, on balance, I come down ever so slightly on the side of hope: I think that given enough time and accurate enough information, people eventually do make wise decisions.

The trouble is that in the present situation, time and useful insight are both in short supply. While we have a window of time left in which to consider the manifold challenges of everyware, and to articulate a meaningful response to them, that window is closing. Ubiquitous computing appears in more places, in more guises, and in more ambitious conceptions with every passing day, and we've barely begun to confront it in the depth of understanding it demands.

The real struggle will be in finding an appropriate place for ubiquitous computing in our lives—reserving it for those applications where it will be able to do us the most good, while ensuring that our more intimate choices and moments remain autonomous and unmediated. The English proverb has it that "the devil is in the details." The architect Mies van der Rohe famously restated this in more optimistic terms; in his version, the details of implementation are precisely where one might go looking for God. In the case of everyware, we can only hope that Mies knew what he was talking about.

New York City/Tokyo/Margaux, FR/Berlin
June 2005—January 2006

Index

M

MacColl, Ian, 137–139
Mainwaring, Scott, 243
Makkuni, Ranjit, 22, 30
Mann, Steve, 50–52, 222
maps
    GAUDI system, 64–65, 79
    Google, 83, 162
    HousingMaps, 162
    public navigation, 63–65
    Semapedia, 210
    zooming in on, 41, 43–44
Marx, Gary T., 109–110, 127–128
mashups, 142, 161–163
Maslow, Abraham, 187
McLuhan, Marshall, 98, 148–149
media table, 41–42
medical providers/medicine, 48–49, 66,
    103, 105
mesh networking, 19, 99, 186
metadata, 23, 162, 184
microcontrollers, 12, 18, 142, 212
microprocessors, 11, 38
military, 52–53, 95
Minority Report, 43, 94–95
MIT Media Lab, 12, 40, 50, 69, 94
mobile phones, 10, 12, 21, 167–169
modularity, 141–143
monitors, 201–203. *See also* screens
Moore's law, 115–117
Morville, Peter, 65
mouse, 41, 42, 112
movies/novels, 93–95
multiplicity, 75–78
Murakami, Teruyasu, 167–168, 259
Museum of Modern Art, New York, 107
Mutanen, Ulla-Maaria, 129

N

Nass, Clifford, 154–155
navigation. *See* maps; transportation
network infrastructure, 186–187
networking
    Bluetooth, 31, 51, 204, 206
    mesh, 19, 99, 186
    PAN, 204–205

ubiquitous, 12
UWB, 99, 204
Wi-Fi, 21, 204–206
New Songdo, South Korea, 218–219
Ning Web service, 162–163
Nomura Research Institute, 104, 167
Nordenson, Guy, 107
Norman, Don, 22, 26, 29, 91
novels/movies, 93–95
NTT DoCoMo, 169

O

Octopus smartcards, 183, 215–217, 259
office environment, 19–20, 54, 57–58. *See
    also* buildings; indoor environment
output devices/methods, 24, 55, 62, 67, 80,
    127, 128
Oxford Union, 250

P

pads, 19–20
Palo Alto Research Center (PARC), 11–15,
    19–22, 29
PAN (personal area networking), 204–205
paradigm shift, 16–17, 30, 35, 87, 89
payment systems
    Blink payment system, 28, 215, 230
    Octopus smartcards, 183, 215–217, 259
    PayPass, 28, 79, 135, 140, 179, 215
people. *See also* user experience; users
    anonymity, 144–145
    children, 66, 105, 249
    disabled, 66, 105
    elderly, 30, 103–106, 238
    everyday life, 18–24, 33–34, 131–133
    faculty atrophy of, 148–151
    human body, 48–53
    human-computer interaction, 14, 70, 196
    personal/recreational activities, 123–125
    social interactions, 84–87, 124, 126,
        154–155
personal computers (PCs), 69, 177–178, 193
personal computing, 11, 37–39, 46, 87, 178.
    See also computing
PetLog (UK), 185

phatic utterances, 132
phones, mobile, 10, 12, 21, 167–169
photo-sharing services, 83, 127
physical computing, 1, 40–41
privacy issues, 2–3, 26, 108, 126–128, 170, 172, 256. *See also* surveillance
processors, 38, 115–117, 193–195
product identifiers, 129–130
public space, 59–65, 107, 143, 172

R

radio-frequency identification. *See* RFID
Reeves, Byron, 154–155
Rekimoto, Jun, 42, 94
relationality, 81–83
remote controls (motes), 12–13, 168, 192
remote systems, 18, 189
RFID tags, 13, 98–99, 185, 209–211, 249
RFID technology, 27, 98–99, 209. *See also* payment systems
Riley, Terence, 107
Robeson, Paul, 125
rooms. *See* indoor environment
Rural Electrification Program, 186
Ryoan-ji temple, Kyoto, 42

S

Saarinen, Eliel, 125
Salt'n'Pepa, 161
Schneier, Bruce, 147*n*
Schulze, Jack, 113–114
Schwartz, Delmore, 222
screens
    computer display, 201–203
    everyware and, 40, 56, 58
    resolution, 201
    wall, 38, 56, 58, 75, 76
seamlessness, 137–140
security, 20, 60, 107–110, 147. *See also* surveillance
Sensacell, 55
SenseWear patch, 26, 49, 79, 150–151
sensors
    biometric, 48–49, 94, 105, 150–151
    floor, 37–38, 54–55, 142, 143, 238

networked, 12, 49, 67, 110
    problems with, 143, 164, 235
    surveillance and, 30
SGML (Standard Generalized Markup Language), 212–214
Small Design Firm, 41
smart buildings, 31, 59–62
smart flooring, 37–38, 54–55, 142, 143, 238
Smart Hydro bathtub, 123
smartcards, 183, 215–217, 259. *See also* payment systems
Snell helmet-certification standards, 255
social interactions, 84–87, 124, 126, 154–155
Social Security numbering system, 145–146
Sony Computer Science Laboratories (CSL), 42
sound. *See* audio
speech output, 44–45, 112, 132–133
Stamen Design, 162
Stanford University, 13, 77, 144
Stiegler, Bernard, 128
storage capacity, 196–198
surveillance, 3, 30, 107–110, 246–249. *See also* privacy issues; security

T

tabs, 19–20
Tactiva, 43
tangible media, 12, 16, 30, 40–45, 57
terrorism, 107–108, 110
Testa, Peter, 62
Thackara, John, 233
ThingLinks, 129
tools, digital, 19, 96–97, 229, 243
Total cost of ownership (TCO), 173
touchpad, 40, 43
trackball, 40, 42
transit pass, 109, 216–217, 243
transportation, 109, 216–217, 219, 248. *See also* maps

U

ubicomp (ubiquitous computing), 11–15, 21, 111, 191
Ubiquitous Communicators (UCs), 167, 177

ADAM GREENFIELD is an internationally recognized user experience consultant and critical futurist, having worked for clients ranging from global concerns like Toyota, Capgemini, and Sony to local nonprofits.

Before starting his current practice, Studies and Observations, Adam was lead information architect for the Tokyo office of well-known Web consultancy Razorfish; prior to that, he worked as senior information architect for marchFIRST, also in Tokyo. At various points in his career, he has also been a rock critic for *SPIN* magazine, a medic at the Berkeley Free Clinic, a coffeehouse owner in West Philadelphia, and a PSYOP sergeant in the Special Operations Command of the U.S. Army.

With a particular interest in the interplay between mobility and the user experience, Adam organized the first international Moblogging Conference in Tokyo in 2003, acclaimed as the world's first symposium devoted to the practice of Web publishing from mobile devices. More recently, Adam sat on the final jury for the Fusedspace competition on novel uses of information technology in public space.

A co-founder of Boxes & Arrows, a Web-based journal on interactive design and information architecture, Adam speaks frequently before a wide variety of audiences on issues of design, culture, technology and user experience. His Chrysler Design Award–nominated personal site can be found at www.v-2.org.

Adam lives and works in New York City with his wife, artist Nurri Kim.